A
MEDIEVAL
BOOK OF
SEASONS

A MEDIEVAL BOOK OF SEASONS

Marie Collins & Virginia Davis

Picture Research by Deborah Pownall

 HarperCollins *Publishers*

To Peter and John

Page 1: Two farm labourers working together, one
with a scythe and one with a pitchfork, with the
products of their labour: neatly ranged haycocks.

Frontispiece: A late fifteenth-century clock face.
Human activities are shown governed by the zodiacal
cycle and seasonal influences.

Contents page: A weary labourer, carrying his scythe,
returns home after a long day's work in the fields.

A MEDIEVAL BOOK OF SEASONS

Copyright © 1992
by Marie Collins and Virginia Davis.

All rights reserved.

Printed in the United Kingdom.

No part of this book may be used or reproduced in
any manner whatsoever without written
permission except in the case of brief quotations
embodied in critical articles and reviews.

For information address
Harper Collins Publishers
10 East 53rd Street, New York, NY 10022.

First U.S. Edition

Designed by Paul Watkins

Printed by Eagle Colourbooks Ltd, Blantyre, Glasgow

Library of Congress Catalog Card Number 91-50462

ISBN 0-06-016 821-8

91   92   93   94   95   96   97   98   99   10   9   8   7   6   5   4   3   2   1

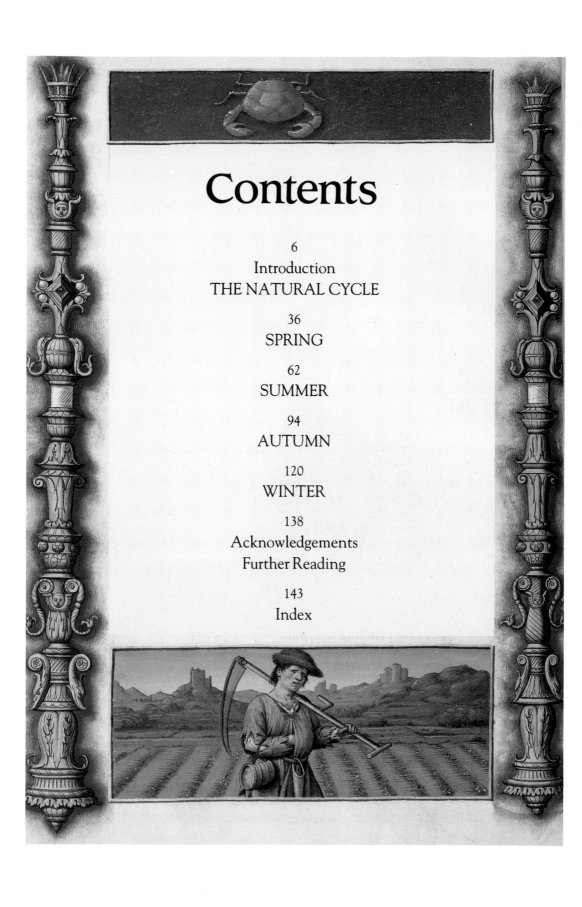

Contents

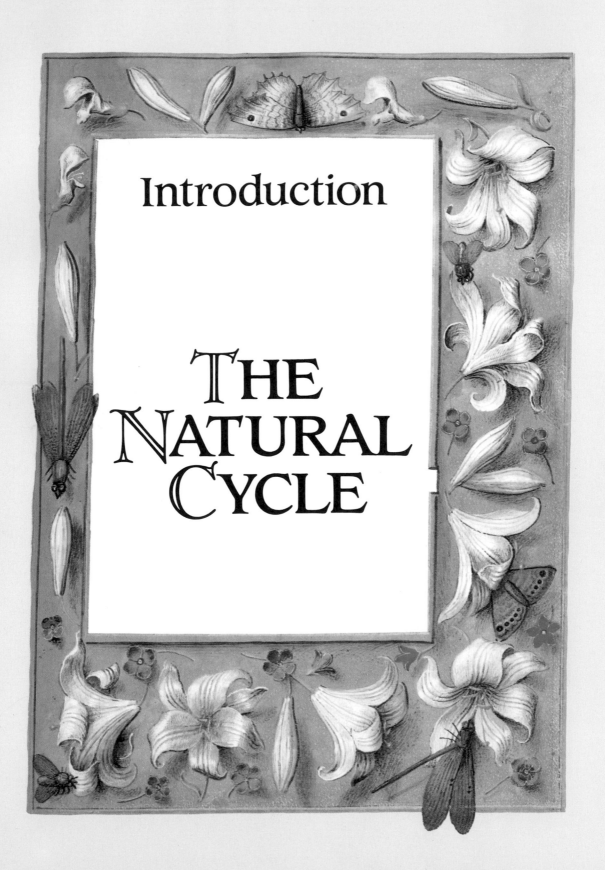

Introduction

THE
NATURAL
CYCLE

Full-page spreads of beautiful and precise paintings of plant and insect life might enrich Books of Hours; here single-flowered roses are shown with a very realistic caterpillar and a clearly-recognizable Red Admiral butterfly

The later middle ages were an exciting and vibrant period – merchants travelled from the east with exotic spices and rich silks, artists developed theories of perspective and exploited new approaches to drawing and painting, enormously innovative and elaborate buildings were designed and built, the universities were expanding, and many other cultural developments came thick and fast. This is not to disguise the fact that there were many unpleasant aspects to life; it could certainly be 'nasty, brutish and short', but the middle ages were not, any more than any other period, a time of unalloyed misery and repression. Given H.G. Wells's time machine, what would strike the modern reader transported back to the fourteenth and fifteenth centuries, the period with which this book is primarily concerned?

The modern reader transported to medieval Europe would find it impossible to explain easily twentieth-century attitudes to time, or modern ways of measuring it both throughout the day and throughout the year. On the one hand, in modern Europe vast expanses of the more backward areas are farmed by country people whose days and years are ruled, much as they were in medieval times, by the amount of daylight available and by the weather, according to the year's natural cycle. On the other hand, the lives of many twentieth-century people, especially city-dwellers, are ruled nowadays, often at a crazy pace, by minute, accurate and universally agreed measurements of time. Medieval country people, by contrast, would have had little beyond the local monastery bell, ringing out the hours of religious services, to mark out the day's divisions. 'Civilized' life as modern city-dwelling Westerners know it would fall apart

A European view of travel to China. Medieval travellers
to the Orient encountered alien and confusing systems
of measuring time

without its rigid frame of shared conventions about measuring time; our travelling arrangements, business procedures, manufacturing processes and communications could not function without precision timing, or without a communally agreed way of dividing up the year. The confusion of crossing the dateline in intercontinental air-travel is a small price to pay for the convenience of having a system of dates on which everyone agrees. Medieval people, by contrast, accustomed to marking out the major events of their lives by reference to church festivals, would have found the modern preoccupation with exact dating bewildering. In much of the modern world, time rules people, rather than the reverse; even our amusements squeeze uncomfortable humour out of our stressful obsession with dates and times, ranging from the White Rabbit's agitation in *Alice in Wonderland* to the paranoia of John Cleese's manic headmaster in the film *Clockwise*.

Our lives nowadays are so bound up with clocks dividing the day into twenty-four equal hours, and with calendars beginning the year on 1 January, that it often comes as a surprise to discover that other cultures and times approached their days and years differently. Occasionally, in our multiracial society, we get a glimpse of different approaches to times and seasons, as when the Chinese New Year is vigorously celebrated with firecrackers and dancing dragons in London's Soho; or when Jewish New Year and Diwali greetings cards appear in our shops; or simply when we take a holiday in a remote area of Europe and realize that for a Greek goatherd or a Sicilian peasant, their life has a completely different rhythm from ours.

The system of counting years from the notional birth of Jesus Christ was not always general in medieval Christian societies. An Englishman, the Northumbrian monk Bede, was responsible for promoting the use of the Christian year, *annus domini* [AD], the 'year of Our Lord' for dating purposes, in Anglo-Saxon England. Gradually in the centuries after Bede's death in 735 it was adopted all over Europe. It was not, however, the only way of reckoning the year and of dating documents in the middle ages. A legacy of the Roman Empire was the unwieldy system of the *indiction*, primarily used by lawyers and at the papal court; it was based on cycles of fifteen years computed from AD 312. Various indictions started the year at other times than 1 January. Many kingdoms used a 'regnal year', starting

A prosperous-looking couple, warmly dressed, on their way to
church, in a late fifteenth-century Flemish illustration

from the day when the king came to the throne. We really have nothing to
complain about nowadays with the international datelines and time-
zones; the lack of standardization of dating *years* in medieval Europe could
cause far worse confusion! The historian R.L. Poole spells out the example
of a traveller going from Venice to France in the thirteenth century who
would pass through several date zones. Setting out from Venice on 1
March 1245, he would find himself in 1244 when he reached Florence and
if, after a short stay, he went on to Pisa, the year 1246 would already have
begun there. Continuing his journey westward he would find himself again
in 1245 when he entered Provence and on arriving in France before Easter
he would be once more in 1244!

Imperial Rome had formalized the division of the year into twelve
months, a system which we essentially retain, but it was difficult to get
one's mind around the system of irregular subdivisions of months. For the
Romans each month was divided into unequal periods of Kalends, Nones
and Ides; the modern way of numbering the days of each month in one
continuous ascending sequence gradually became dominant during the
middle ages. But the most important calendar in the middle ages was that
of the church. Days of the year were consecrated as festivals of particular
saints; these became very important for dating both public and private
events, whether the death of a king or the birth of a peasant baby. Saints'
days were fixed, i.e. they fell on the same date each year; other church
feasts, in particular those relating to events in Christ's life, were movable,

depending on the variable date of Easter. Calculating the date of Easter,
the principal festival of the Christian year which provided the starting-
point for fixing all the other movable feasts, was a major operation; it
involved the use of complex tables based on a factor known as the Golden
Number, and on the lunar year (the year as divided up according to the
thirteen cycles of the moon).

Fortunately, few medieval men and women outside royal and papal
government, or the world of scholarship, had to concern themselves with
the detailed complexities of different dating systems which were a
headache for church authorities and official scribes. For many, the year
was dictated by the rhythms of the seasons, intertwined with the pattern of
the Christian year. The year's cycle was marked by farming activities and
by religious and worldly feasts and festivals. People's lack of awareness of a
calendar, in the sense in which we understand it, can be seen in legal cases
where proof of age was necessary. This was done by reference, not to
particular years, but to momentous events in the memories of village
elders. William le Marchal of Kingston Stanley in Gloucestershire
produced eleven witnesses to the fact that he was over twenty-one and had
been baptized on Thursday 8 May 1309; their testimony included the
following vivid recollections of other personal events used as points of
reference for the memory: 'John le Weler says that on the Friday following
[William's baptism], Elizabeth his sister fell into a certain marlpit and
broke her neck; Hugh de Dodebrugg says that on the Monday next before
that Thursday, Adam his son became a friar at the house of St Augustine in
Oxenford; Richard Pynock says that on that Thursday he lifted from the
font in the church…John son of William Dispenser who was baptized in
the same water in which the said William was baptized.'

Although nowadays the course of the seasons can still affect our urban
lives practically to a limited degree, we are cushioned to a great extent
against all but severe extremes. Roused by alarm clocks in our centrally-
heated bedrooms before dawn has broken, helped by household
technology to wash in hot water and to feed ourselves quickly and
conveniently, we can comfortably walk along an electrically lit metalled
road to the train or bus and go into work for our usual time, summer or
winter. The seasons do not affect the rhythm of the day for a large number
of modern people. For medieval people, by contrast, the rhythms of the

Upper: Under the zodiacal sign of Aries (the Ram), vines are
being pruned in March

seasons were reflected even in the smaller units of time of which people
were conscious in ordinary life, the days and hours. Until the mid-
fourteenth century at least, days were not divided up into twenty-four
hours of equal length. The amount of daylight in any one day varies with
the season, so dividing the available daylight into equal divisions, 'solar
hours', meant that the hour itself was of variable length from day to day
and season to season. A summer hour, one twelfth of the available
daylight, was much longer than a winter hour, until the advent of the
mechanical clock dividing the day into precisely measured and equal units
of time. The change to mechanically measured equal hours was probably
welcome to fourteenth-century schoolchildren and students, for whom an
early summer class or lecture had been considerably longer than a winter
one, under the variable solar time system! The sub-divisions of the day also
bore some relation, in their names if not in practical fact, to the monastic
divisions of the religious day at which services were said (to express
midday, 'noon' from 'Nones', the name of a monastic service, still survives
in modern English). When artificial light was rare and costly, the day's
routines, especially outdoor activities, were necessarily governed by the
availability of daylight which varied with the season. By modern
standards, work began very early in the morning, most commonly at Prime
(approximately 6 a.m.); most sales and trade activities were forbidden
before Prime. Medieval people were habitually 'summoned by bells'
announcing publicly the customary or permitted times for their activities,
like the masons of fourteenth-century York, whose 'times and hours' were
to be 'ruled by a bell ordained therefore'. In winter, outdoor activities
necessarily ended earlier than in summer, but local government
regulations stipulated the hours when work must cease for the day; these
varied according to one's craft, which sometimes caused complaint when
the trade was noisy, as with London's wiremongers, who were allowed to
work only until 9 p.m. in summer and 8 p.m. in winter to avoid annoyance
to their neighbours. The curfew-bell (from French 'couvre-feu', 'cover,
i.e. put out, the fire'), initially a fire-precaution, would have told workers
when to stop; in most places the curfew-bell rang at 8 p.m. in winter and 9
p.m. in summer.

  The different characters of the seasons were clearly appreciated in the
middle ages and can be found expressed in the writings of many medieval

Lower: Under the zodiacal sign of Libra (the Scales),
grapes are being trodden in October

authors, both scholars and poets. One of the clearest descriptions of the course of the seasons appears in the many medieval versions and translations of the *Secretum Secretorum* or 'Secret of Secrets', a twelfth- or early thirteenth-century Latin translation of a tenth-century Arabic treatise on government and statecraft. It included a great deal of other very miscellaneous lore and was widely known; Chaucer very probably took many details of his famous 'spring' passage opening the Prologue to his *Canterbury Tales* from it. The *Secretum Secretorum*, with its remarkable assembly of fascinating facts and pseudo-science, did not long remain locked away for the few in Latin, the language of scholarship. Various translations exist into several medieval European languages, making its content much more accessible. A fifteenth-century Middle English translation now in the Bodleian Library, Oxford, provides definitions of the seasons' durations, speaking in terms both of calendar dates and of astrological designations:

Of Ver [Spring]: Ver begins when the sun enters the sign of Aries, and lasts ninety-three days, twenty-three hours and fifteen minutes, that is to say, it begins on the eleventh day of March and ends on the thirteenth day of June. At its beginning, day and night are of equal length...

Of Summer: Summer begins when the sun enters the sign of the Crab, and lasts ninety-three days, nine hours and twenty minutes, that is to say, it begins on the thirteenth day of June and lasts until the fourteenth day of September. At this time the days are at their longest, and nights in all regions grow shorter...

Of Harvest [Autumn]: Harvest begins when the sun enters the sign of Libra and contains eighty-nine days and six hours. This is from the fourteenth day of September until the twelfth day of December. At this time, days and nights are of equal length... and during this period the night grows longer...

Of Winter: Winter begins when the sun enters the sign of Capricorn and contains eighty-eight days, fifteen hours and fourteen minutes, that is to say, from the twelfth day of December until the eleventh day of March. At this time the night is longest and the days are shortest...

Other versions of the *Secretum*, which, like most medieval works, was adapted and altered by successive users and rewriters, give slightly different dates, but essentially the seasons are thought of as divisions of the year reflecting nature's four major periods: new growth, florescence, fruition and decline. The *Secretum* also describes the physical world of creation as conceived of by medieval scholars; they saw clear parallels and interrelationships between the structure of the whole creation (the macrocosm) and that of man (the microcosm). The world, according to scholars, was made up of the four 'elements', fire, air, water and earth. These 'elements' were produced by the mingling of the four principal 'contrary qualities', heat, cold, moisture and dryness. Fire was hot and dry, air was hot and moist, water was cold and moist, and earth was cold and dry. Man's physical make-up offered a parallel to these combinations; in the human body the four principal contrary qualities combined to form the four constituent 'humours', or substances which influenced a person's physical and mental make-up: blood, choler, phlegm, and melancholy or black bile. The qualities of heat and moisture combined to make blood, which, if it dominated in a person, caused the positive 'sanguine' temperament of which we still speak; heat and dryness made choler, the rather negative and angry 'choleric' temperament; cold and dryness made melancholy, the negative, obsessive, depressive and brooding temperament; cold and moisture made phlegm, the repellently dull and apathetic temperament. In the medieval view, one's 'temperament' or 'complexion', that is, one's basic nature, depended on the proportions in which these humours were blended; one humour usually predominated, so that a person could be described as an essentially 'sanguine', 'choleric', 'phlegmatic' or 'melancholic' type. The links between the changes of seasons and times in the external world, and the changes taking place in human bodies and moods, were felt to be very close. At different seasons of the year and times of the day, the different humours were thought to dominate. The sanguine temperament was dominant in spring, and from midnight to 6 a.m. each day; the choleric in summer, and from 6 a.m. to noon; the melancholic in autumn, and from noon to 6 p.m.; and the phlegmatic in winter, and from 6 p.m. to midnight. By this theory the best times of the year were early spring mornings, and the worst late winter evenings; on commonsense grounds, one could hardly fault this!

A homely depiction of the element water, here poured
out by Aquarius, the water-carrier of the Zodiac

An early morning scene in a peasant house. Life side-by-side
with the animals was noisy and smelly

The modern time traveller transported back to the late middle ages
might be particularly struck, at a personal level, by the medieval lack of
privacy. This was the case at all levels of society. Peasant families were
likely to live in one-roomed, wattle and daub thatched cottages, often in
close proximity to their animals. Archaeological evidence suggests that
many peasant dwellings of the 'longhouse' type were built to house humans
at one end and animals at the other end of the same long chamber; the
bodies of the livestock often provided a source of warmth in winter. At
higher levels of society too, however, there was also a lack of privacy; great
nobles were not often alone but were constantly surrounded by courtiers
and servants. Even the bedchamber would not offer much solitude; it was
likely also to be used as a room in which to conduct business. The more
humble members of a great household would sleep on straw palliasses in
communal rooms. It was also difficult to escape the elements and the more
unpleasant side of life. While grand castle or manor walls might be hung
with lavish tapestries which went some way towards keeping out the
draughts, other rooms were frequently cold and damp. One French poet's
description of the miseries of the French court in winter quoted on
p.125 rings true; how much worse it must have been for many peasants.
Even when fuel was plentiful, fires created an atmosphere which must

For the well-off, winter's miseries were mitigated by warm fires
and comfortable rooms. Here the window is glazed and the bed
surrounded by rich hangings

often have been smoky and unpleasant. Poor-quality candles provided
more fumes than light and did little to brighten gloomy buildings in
the dark days of winter. All these factors combined to ensure that the
rhythm of life was closely dictated by the seasons and the availability of
natural light.

The smells which were generated by a mass of humans and animals
living in close proximity to each other in medieval dwellings with few
washing facilities and scant sanitation can only be imagined. The problem
continued unabated into more modern times: in the early eighteenth
century, courtiers at the lavish palace built by Louis XIV at Versailles
complained that there were not enough privies for them to use and that
courtiers had to relieve themselves in corners. Medieval privies were
certainly no more plentiful or hygienic.

In the twentieth century, we shy away from dirt, smells and disease;
death has become almost a taboo subject. In the middle ages both birth
and death were closer to everyday life than is the case today. Infant
mortality was high and the lifespan for those who survived infancy might
well be short. Certainly some people lived to great ages, although they
were often rich ecclesiastics who were better nourished than the mass of
the populace and who might be protected by their occupation from some of

Left: Poppies, the source of opiate painkillers, were often
illustrated in herbals describing the medicinal properties of
plants, as in this beautiful Italian example. Right: A physician
treats his patient for an ugly-looking leg injury

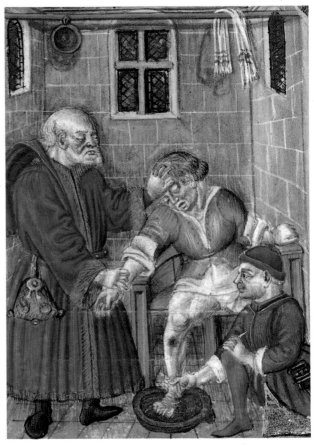

the more violent aspects of medieval life. For women there were particular
risks of dying in childbirth; for men injuries at work or in warfare were
particular problems. The dangers of everyday life are clear from a reading
of coroners' records, which show a wide variety of fatal mishaps: violent
death in a tavern brawl; accidental drowning in moats or millponds; being
trampled by a runaway animal; a fatal blow on the head during a rough
village game, to name but a few. Warfare too, a way of life for the noble
classes all over Europe, was a dangerous activity, not simply or even
primarily because of the danger of death in battle, but because of the
'occupational hazards' of military life. Many injuries, such as a kick from a
frightened horse being loaded on to a boat, took place on campaign, and
brutal fights often broke out among a force of men kept together for
lengthy periods. Minor injuries which remained inadequately treated, or
the dysentery which was rife in army camps, might well prove fatal.

Men lie dying beside a procession of churchmen and lay people
praying for deliverance from the plague in Rome. Epidemics
were seen as God's punishment for human wickedness; hence
the hooded flagellants scourge each other in penance

Wealth or social status did not protect one from such dangers; King Henry
V of England died of dysentery on campaign in France.

Surviving treatises and medical textbooks testify to the medieval
interest in medical matters, but treatment was often not efficacious. What
few effective treatments there were came from medicaments derived from
herbs and medicinal plants; knowledge of these practical remedies was
often preserved by women and by monks. Frequent blood-letting, a very
common practice, weakened rather than assisted a patient's recovery.
What is perhaps most alarming about medieval medicine to the modern
mind is the awful prospect of unhygienic and unanaesthetized operations
carried out with the fiendish-looking instruments illustrated in medical
manuals of the time. The intervention of a doctor was often more likely to
hasten death than assist recovery.

Awareness of death, always close, was strengthened from the middle of the fourteenth century by the arrival in Europe of bubonic plague, carried there from the east by the fleas who lived on the black rat. The first and worst outbreak of plague, the Black Death of 1347–9, is often portrayed as a watershed in European history – more than a third of the population died during this period. The long-term effects of this huge disaster were worsened by the repeated return of the plague in the remainder of the fourteenth and fifteenth centuries; it killed fewer people on subsequent visitations than on the first one but none the less effectively kept the population down. The realization that death could strike suddenly encouraged some rich people to prepare themselves for death by endowing lavish chantry chapels, where priests would pray for their souls, while some poorer people joined local guilds or confraternities (pious societies) where they vowed to pray for one another's souls.

The middle ages are often portrayed as an era dominated by a repressive Catholic church, corrupt and in need of reform. Yet what would strike the modern time-traveller visiting late medieval Europe would not be the oppressiveness of the church, but rather, the wide acceptance of religion as a normal part of everyday life. People attended mass regularly; this was a normal part of existence, rather than an imposition. Religion was closely interwoven with daily life; sermons by travelling friars were popular occasions, and itinerant players performed plays with religious and moral themes. Holy days were welcome holidays. In villages the church was at the centre of community life. Local religious houses provided valuable social services to the community, perhaps running small schools, providing rudimentary nursing care and giving food and shelter to travellers. Well-off widows might aspire to spend their latter days in the relatively secure environment of a convent. Many people were concerned about the fate of their immortal souls and took care to provide for their welfare, though others carried out their religious commitments sketchily, trusting that the church would save them.

Travel and communication were at once arduous and frequent in the middle ages. In many areas of Europe roads were of poor quality; main trade routes might be well maintained, but tracks between rural settlements were often rough, perhaps becoming impassable in winter. The pneumatic tyre is an invention of the late nineteenth century; in the middle ages wheels were fashioned from the wood of springy saplings, but even the best

An aristocratic group enjoys a spring ride

wheelwrights could do little to compensate for the poor quality of the roads. Transport of heavy goods was difficult; many small-time merchants hawked their goods from village to village on pack animals.

Such difficulties did not, however, deter those who wanted to travel either for business purposes or for pleasure. Many medieval men and women were on the move, fulfilling business commitments, travelling in search of a job or on central or local government business. Pilgrimages were popular, admittedly with an ostensibly religious objective, but also attractive because of the excitement and the pleasure of travelling. Men and women were stirred by the excitement of seeing new places and

This fowler, shown here approaching a walled town, may
or may not have come by his catch legitimately. Lower:
The Archbishop of Canterbury, Thomas Arundel,
supporting the cause of King Henry IV of England,
who deposed King Richard II in 1399

meeting new people. Some pilgrims travelled vast distances – the most adventurous to Jerusalem or Rome, others merely to local shrines. Travelling could of course be dangerous, and even the wealthy, who might be cushioned from some of the more uncomfortable aspects of travel, found themselves at risk from robbers and outlaws or from natural dangers. Sea-crossing was a dangerous activity, as many government officials commuting between England and the continent or England and Ireland found – fatalities included an Archbishop of Dublin, drowned while crossing the Irish Sea, and the son of King Henry I, drowned when his ship, the ill-fated White Ship, went down in the Channel.

Travellers carried news and information from place to place. The pedlars who wandered from village to village were a lively source of information about the outside world. Communication was a problem in the middle ages (in the nature of things, it could not be very speedy); for example, it took about six weeks for the momentous news of the fall of Constantinople to the Turks to reach Rome in 1453, and longer still to get to England. Kings made some attempts to establish rapid communications networks, but they were hampered by the vagaries of the wind in sea travel, by the poor quality of roads and bridges, and sometimes by outlaws and bandits in remote regions like the Apennines. Much information was disseminated through the church in sermons and in proclamations made to the assembled villagers. Popular ballads and songs, which spread rapidly, often celebrated and commemorated great events.

Kings were not blind to the value of spreading political propaganda, not so much using mass media as by more subtle means: for example, coronation ceremonies emphasized the power and authority of the king. The spread of the idea that the kings of England and France had the healing touch, the power to heal scrofula (a tubercular disease causing hideous skin eruptions), enhanced their power still further. News of victories in battles was rapidly disseminated; the church had its part to play, as bishops ordered prayers of thanksgiving to be offered up in local churches. Processions and parades had propaganda value, as had great building projects and lavish expenditure upon works of art.

In the early middle ages literacy was viewed with some suspicion; actions definitely spoke louder than words, especially written words. It was not always seen as necessary to have transactions recorded in writing.

Opposite: A peasant digging his plot doffs his hat to the lady of
the manor. A moated manor-house, approached by a
drawbridge, is in the background

These attitudes changed as the middle ages progressed; government
became more dependent on records, and correspondingly the rest of
society became increasingly aware that memories were not enough. It
became important to have written proof of ownership or events. Latin was
the language of government and official business, but by the fourteenth
century an increasing amount of writing was being conducted in the
vernacular. The growth of international business networks was important
in encouraging both the growth of a literate trading class and the
development of sophisticated accounting systems such as double-entry
book-keeping. The oral tradition remained strong, but as the middle ages
progressed, reading or listening to other people reading became a more
widespread leisure activity among the upper ranks of society. Particularly
popular as entertainment were romances, and tales of the heroes of the
past; for the devout, Books of Hours helped men and women to pray at
home. Lavishly illustrated Books of Hours provide many of the
illustrations in the present book.

Rural society was the norm in late medieval Europe. With the
significant exceptions of northern Italy and the Netherlands, where far
more of the population lived in towns, most people lived in isolated
villages in rural areas. The social structure was hierarchical. At the apex of
the feudal pyramid were the king and the great barons, and below them, a
mass of landowners of various sizes and with a number of civil duties. Some
were substantial landholders, with several manors in different parts of the
country; others were less well-off, with only a single manor. Land was the
basis of wealth. The vast majority of the population was composed of the
peasants and serfs who lived on the land, but within this general group
there were various gradations, from the richer village peasants, whose
prosperity led them to resent their obligations to do service to the lord of
the manor, down to the landless labourer, who scraped a living where he
could.

The agricultural year, consisting of four unequal sections, began and
ended at Michaelmas (29 September), by which time the last of the
harvest should have been in. Manorial accounts, which give detailed
pictures of agricultural activity on the manors they describe, worked on a
Michaelmas-to-Michaelmas basis. On the estates of the bishop of
Chichester, for example, winter was taken as the season from Michaelmas

The months and their labours. A fifteenth-century French
illustration of an agricultural treatise by a fourteenth-century
Italian naturalist, Peter of Crescenzi

to Christmas; the term 'Lent' roughly applied to the period from the end of
the Christmas festival to Holy Week; summer lasted from Hocktide, after
Holy Week, to Lammas or 'Loaf-Mass' (1 August) when the communion
bread was baked with the first-fruits of the harvest; while the period
between Lammas and Michaelmas was described as autumn or harvest-
time.

It is hardly surprising that poets, scholars and farmers, with their
different experiences, thought differently about the extent, nature and
activities of the seasons; it is equally unsurprising that poets setting literary
fashions in one particular country should describe a season in ways not

matching up to the practical experience of poets imitating their works in other countries and climates. The traditional Labours of the Months (the conventional activities of each month as depicted in art and literature) could hardly have been the same in practical terms from England or north Germany right down to Tuscany or Sicily, yet their regional differences, as represented in art and literature, are far slighter than might be expected. Fashion and convention were very powerful forces in the arts.

The Labours of the Months were an adapted classical legacy, derived from the series of activities and mythological figures depicted on Roman calendars; the medieval versions have a Christian basis, often implicit rather than explicit. They depend upon a scheme of things in which God has ordained that in this changeable world, 'To everything there is a season, and a time to every purpose under the heaven: a time to be born, and a time to die; a time to plant, and a time to pluck up that which is planted' (Ecclesiastes iii. 1–2). A rhyme from a later fifteenth-century manuscript now in the Bodleian Library, Oxford, presents a typical version of the conventional Labours of the Months depicted throughout Europe in art and literature.

January	By this fire I warm my hands,
February	And with my spade I delve my lands.
March	Here I set my things to spring,
April	And here I hear the birds sing.
May	I am light as bird on bough,
June	And I weed my corn well enow.
July	With my scythe my mead I mow,
August	And here I shear my corn full low.
September	With my flail I earn my bread,
October	And here I sow my wheat so red.
November	At Martinmas I kill my swine,
December	And at Christmas I drink red wine.

The monthly activities listed are surprisingly consistent and conventional across a wide area of Europe, despite the climatic and geographical differences which affected the routine of occupations in different regions and countries. In January it was cold in much of Europe,

A superb landscape is the background to a November Labour of the Month, as the village swineherds fatten their pigs. This illustration comes from the late fifteenth-century completion by Jean Colombe of the famous *Très riches heures* of the Duc de Berry, left uncompleted by the Limburg brothers after their patron's death

so it is not remarkable to find its dominant activity illustrated almost everywhere as warming oneself by the fire, or feasting. Where January shows feasting, toasting oneself by the fire tends to appear in February. March frequently shows digging or pruning; April, with a flower-bearing figure, and May, with a rider, return to leisure and pleasure. Most of the Labours of the Months, however, depict work rather than amusements. In Italy, France and Spain, reaping is found illustrated as a principal labour of June and July, whereas in Germany and England it tends to be placed in July and August, perhaps a sporadic reflection of reality instead of a pictorial convention. Threshing, too, comes later in English illustrations (usually under September) than in Italian, French and Spanish series, where it tends to be placed in July and August. On the continent,

A reaper working hard in the heat of the summer

September and October are above all the months for illustrating the vintage with the picking and treading of grapes followed by the filling of casks with wine. English manuscripts illustrate the wine-harvest, too; viticulture was possible, though not cost-effective, in late medieval England, becoming increasingly uneconomic once abundant and reasonably-priced wines were available from the Bordeaux region; by the sixteenth century English-grown grapes were unusual enough to excite comment. October, November and December are mainly devoted to providing for the winter in various ways, particularly by feeding up and subsequently slaughtering pigs and oxen and by gathering wood. The declining months of the year are also illustrated by ploughing and sowing, aimed at providing next year's early cereal harvest. December shares its other major activity, feasting, with January; the Christmastide festival is shown as taken very seriously in gastronomic terms.

Although the Labours of the Months were widely stereotyped, this did not spoil their impact, to judge from the popularity and frequency of their motifs, particularly in psalters and Books of Hours commissioned for aristocrats at prayer. The demand for illustrations of the Labours of the Months allowed painters with an increasing eye for landscape and naturalistic detail to offer delicate and precise observation of nature and the seasons to delight their aristocratic patrons. Desire for possession of highly decorated Books of Hours was so widespread among the upper and middle classes, in the later middle ages, that it was satirized in contemporary poetry:

> A Book of Hours, too, must be mine,
> Where subtle workmanship will shine,
> Of gold and azure, rich and smart,
> Arranged and painted with great art,
> Covered with fine brocade of gold,
> And there must be, so as to hold
> The pages closed, two golden clasps.

This description successfully conveys the aesthetic pleasure to be gained from the ownership and use of a richly illustrated prayer book. They were the best-selling books of the later middle ages, all over Europe, outselling any other text, religious or secular.

Despite the richness of her setting, this Virgin from the Forster
Book of Hours, tenderly holding her child, makes divine love
seem accessible to ordinary mortals. On the left, a devout
figure, probably the commissioner of the book, is being
presented to the Virgin by St. James, identified by his
traditional cockle shell

It was not just vanity or acquisitiveness which led people to desire Books of Hours. The later middle ages saw a powerful intensification of piety and devotion amongst lay people; many, especially women, were anxious to imitate the clergy in saying the divine services at the appointed 'canonical hours' of each day. Few lay people would go as far as reciting all the services required of monks and priests, but many were anxious to possess their own prayer books; they wanted to be able to perform private devotions at home, as well as to use their books at mass. There was particular devotion to the Virgin Mary; she was seen as more powerful than the saints but, as a human being, less awesome than God and therefore more approachable. Books of Hours centred on the Virgin Mary, with the Hours or Mass of the Virgin, and a number of prayers directed to her, as their focus. These devotional works were not just kept for show but were widely used; many portraits show women at prayer, with Books of Hours in their hands.

Although the Books of Hours are rich in incidental material about the course of life and time in this world, paradoxically they also underline the medieval preoccupation with eternal life, life beyond and outside time. The aim of every Christian soul was, ideally, to live such a life on earth, subject to the limitations of time and mortality, that the prize of eternal blessedness in heaven, freed from time and death, would be won. Because to God, outside time, all earthly times are as one, what might look like anachronism to us was not inappropriate to medieval religious artists. In the fifteenth-century Book of Hours of Isabella Stuart, Duchess of Brittany, the Duchess kneels before the Virgin and Child, to whom she is being presented by St Catherine; such 'anachronistic' presentation-scenes are common, and pious in intent. The desire to transcend time and remind the reader of eternity leads to a rather tasteless and arrogant excess in the case of the *Grandes Heures* of John, Duke of Berry, commissioned during the Duke's lifetime; the Duke is prophetically portrayed as being received and led in at the gate of heaven by (an admittedly rather grudging-looking!) Saint Peter.

Books of Hours were lavishly illustrated; their paintings are both attractive and informative about the medieval world. Scenes illustrating the main part of the text, although often showing religious themes, provide valuable evidence about costume and other aspects of everyday life. Where the angel appears to tell the shepherds of Christ's birth, we see

In the Playfair Book of Hours, the shepherds, amazed at the angel's announcement of Christ's birth, are pictured as rough countrymen surrounded by their flocks. One holds bagpipes, a typical rustic musical instrument

medieval shepherds portrayed with their flocks; where the Virgin is seated indoors, we get a glimpse of the interior of a medieval house. Borders surrounding the text or illustrations are often magnificently painted with animals, flowers or rural scenes. Particularly valuable for their illustrations are the opening pages of any Book of Hours, the Calendar pages, listing the 365 feast days. Often a double page spread for each of the twelve months includes both an illustration of the appropriate sign of the zodiac and a depiction of the rural labour of the month. Although the resulting pictures are often idealized – the grape harvest is rich and rosy, the pig being slaughtered is well fattened, the corn has ripened well, there is a good fire to sit at in winter – they provide unparalleled evidence of agricultural practices, many of which are described but not illustrated in the more prosaic farming manuals and account-books. Although Books of Hours were often owned by town-dwellers, urban surroundings were rarely portrayed in these devotional works. This tendency to favour portrayal of the countryside is a powerful indication of the close self-identification, even of town-dwellers, with rural activities throughout the medieval seasons.

It is with rural life that this book is primarily concerned; with the realities of daily life at the different seasons of the medieval year. What was grown when and where; what were the different seasonal preoccupations of countrymen and women in the Europe of the later middle ages? Some activities were tied closely to the natural cycle and differ little from today – lambs are born in spring, hay is cut in June. Others differ more fundamentally; it is no longer necessary to slaughter animals as winter approaches because they cannot be housed and fed over the winter months. Europe in the later middle ages was a society very different from ours, but yet the range of human emotions expressed in the literature of the period – joy at the onset of spring, despair in winter, grief at the death of a loved one, pleasure in a summer picnic – shows that there are many points of contact between the past and the present, between the world of the later middle ages and that of the late twentieth century.

SPRING

Opposite: This pair of lovers on horseback would doubtless
have agreed with the view expressed in the *Secretum Secretorum*
that 'no season of the year is better than spring'

Spring was the season most extensively celebrated by medieval writers. As defined by the *Secretum Secretorum*, spring began when the sun entered the sign of Aries in mid-March and ended when it entered the sign of Cancer in mid-June. Its characteristics are described as delightful:

The air waxes clear, the winds blow softly, snows dissolve, rivers run. Springs surge up among the mountains, moisture is drawn to the tree-top, branches bud, seeds sprout, grains spring, meadows grow green. Flowers are fair and fresh, trees are clad with new leaves, and the soil is arrayed with herbs and grasses. Beasts beget offspring, pastures are covered with growth and resume a new vigour, birds sing, and the nightingale's song sounds and re-echoes. The earth puts on its full and entire raiment and beauty, and looks like a lovely bride and a very fair maiden adorned with jewels and clad in many colours to appear in men's sight on her wedding-day.

The hot, moist yet temperate conditions of spring, corresponding to the element air and the bodily humour blood (characteristic of the fortunate 'sanguine' temperament) favour certain human activities in diet and hygiene:

And in [spring] the blood is moved, and it is diffused throughout all the parts of the body, and this profits all things that are equal and balanced in their complexions, that is to say, temperate. And so must thy diet be in that season. Italians are accustomed then to eat chickens, curlews, eggs (not above five at a meal) and wild plants that the Arabs call 'scariole', and they are then in the habit of drinking goats' milk. No season of the year is better than [spring].

Spring activities recommended by the *Secretum Secretorum* for healthy living are blood-letting, sexual intercourse (spring is the only season in which lovemaking gets an unconditional go-ahead!), baths, drinking spiced concoctions to stimulate digestion and using purgatives. Any errors or excesses in one's health regime will be compensated for in spring, which offers conditions generally favourable to the human frame.

The beauty and brightness of spring, so enthusiastically celebrated by medieval authors, offered irresistible opportunities to visual artists too: indulging the tendency to see human emotions reflected in natural surroundings, both writers and painters made the most of every chance to relate spring's vigour and loveliness to people's sense of coming alive again after winter's troubles and discomforts. Spring was above all the season of youth and joy: in the vernal garden of the famous thirteenth-century allegorical poem, *The Romance of the Rose*, for example, there was no place for Old Age, painted on the outside of the enclosing garden wall, among other unhappy outcasts from the medieval youth-culture. As in nature the birds and beasts, driven by instinct, were pairing and mating in the kinder weather of spring, so, in the human sphere, young men and girls sought their ideal companions; a spring setting is almost obligatory for medieval literary portrayals of the pursuit of love, whether successful or unsuccessful.

The first and most direct appeal of spring is to the sense of physical well-being and joy in pleasant surroundings shared by animals and humans:

> Sumer is icumen in –
> Lhude sing! cuccu.
> Groweth sed and bloweth med
> And springth the wude nu –
> Sing cuccu.
> [Spring (=*sumer*) has come – sing loudly, cuckoo! The seed is growing, the meadow is in flower, and now the woodland is coming into leaf – sing, cuckoo!]

The joyous swing of the surviving music for this round expresses the seemingly endless energy and productivity of spring, as the song continues with the ewe bleating maternally for her lamb, the cavortings of bullocks and bucks, and the hope that the cuckoo will never fall silent.

Out of sight of the village, a young lover behaves rather
forwardly with the girl of his choice, who appears more
interested in her bagpipes. Lower: With their attendants out
of earshot, these aristocratic lovers relax on cushions in a
flowery glade. Both are richly dressed and sport the elaborate
headgear which was the height of fashion

An idealized picture of rabbits in a warren. Many lords ensured
an ample supply of rabbits by maintaining warrens
on their lands

Delight in the contrast between the pleasantness of spring and the discomfort of winter is common, as in this poem from the collection of medieval lyrics known as the *Carmina Burana*:

> Now, Winter, yieldeth all thy dreariness,
> The cold is over, all thy frozenness,
> All frost and fog, and wind's untowardness.
> All sullenness, uncomely sluggishness,
> Paleness and anger, grief and haggardness.
>
> Comes now the spring with all her fair arrays,
> Never a cloud to stain the shining days:
> Sparkle at night the starry Pleiades.
> Now is the time come of all graciousness,
> Now is the fairest time of gentilesse.

Chaucer, in his poem *The Book of the Duchess*, an elegy for Blanche, Duchess of Lancaster, describes a beautiful dream landscape which 'had

A pastoral idyll: shepherds celebrate spring with music in a
flowery meadow. One plays a flute, the other a jew's harp

forgotten the poverty which winter had made it suffer with its cold
mornings and its sorrows'; again, in his courtly prologue to *The Legend of
Good Women*, he speaks of the earth forgetting the poor condition caused
by the ravages of winter, which had made it naked and destitute, afflicting
it very grievously with its 'sword of cold'.

From the joys of nature to the joys of love is but a short step. One
medieval English poet moves quickly from an economical introductory
sketch of the burgeoning season to his own devotion to the dark-browed,
dark-eyed, smiling Alison: 'Between March and April, when the twig
begins to come into leaf, the little bird delights to sing in her own
language. I live in amorous longing for the fairest of all creatures; she can
bring me joy. . .'

T. S. Eliot has taught the modern reader to think of April as

> . . . the cruellest month, breeding
> Lilacs out of the dead land, mixing
> Memory and desire, stirring
> Dull roots with spring rain.

For the medieval poet, it was almost always May which was the month to awaken exhilarating or disturbing passions, for good or ill, with its standard literary accompaniments (regardless of seasonal local realities): birdsong (especially the nightingale's), sprouting leaves, blossom and gentle warmth. Happy lovers were in harmony with their surroundings; for the unsuccessful, the season's reminders of nature's impulses towards procreation and productivity were all too painful. One early Middle English poem expresses such suffering with economical force: 'The birds are in the woodland, the fish are in the water, and I must go mad; I toss about restlessly for the sake of the best lady of flesh and blood.'

Another medieval English spring poem tells of a lover who observes in unusually naturalistic detail the plants and flowers (daisies, woodruff, wild roses, lilies, fennel and chervil), the nightingale's song, the courting of wild ducks and animals, even down to the humble worms; if he fails to get his girl he will give up 'this wealth of joys' and take to the woods as a fugitive. He seems to forget that the reminders will be just as potent and painful there! A more touching example of forlorn love occurs in a poem from the collection of medieval Latin lyrics known as the 'Cambridge Songs', in which a girl describes her sense of alienation from the beautiful scenes around her:

> Softly the west wind blows;
> Gaily the warm sun goes;
> The earth her bosom sheweth,
> And with all sweetness floweth . . .
>
> I see it with my eyes,
> I hear it with my ears,
> But in my heart are sighs,
> And I am full of tears.
>
> Alone with thought I sit,
> And blench, remembering it;
> Sometimes I lift my head,
> I neither hear nor see . . .

As medieval poets used nature to express their own preoccupations, so they projected their own feelings and behaviour on to nature in many poems depicting creatures, usually birds, discussing their loves, hopes and

A May Day boating party is entertained by music. In honour of
the season the boat is decorated with may-branches. On the far
bank a group of men is out hawking

disappointments. One of the finest of these is Chaucer's dream-poem *The
Parliament of Birds*, in which an assembly of birds representative of all
'social ranks' meets, presided over by Dame Nature, for each to choose a
mate on St Valentine's Day. The festival is described as a gentle spring
day, nothing like the wintry conditions of a normal English February;
realism is sacrificed to literary convention, which requires that discussions
of love take place against a spring-like backdrop.

The coincidence of regenerative themes in certain feasts of the church's
calendar with the regrowth of the natural world in spring did not pass
unnoticed in literature and art. The ecclesiastical year began, not in
spring, but in the declining phase of nature's cycle, with Advent, a
penitential season containing the four Sundays preceding Christmas.
Advent led, by way of Epiphany, into Lent, the period of self-denial
preceding the movable feast of Easter. Lent, coinciding with the
deprivations and discomforts of late winter, was always likely to be lean
and miserable, whatever its precise dates, while the regenerative theme of
Easter, the time of Christ's Resurrection and the occasion for renewed
hopes of salvation for the penitent Christian, coincided with signs of
revival in nature and the beginnings of better weather. Yet more direct
parallels between growth and productivity in the religious and in the
natural year were to be found in the Feast of the Annunciation,
celebrating the Archangel Gabriel's message to Mary that she would bear
the Son of God, and fixed on 25 March, nine calendar months before

Christmas. The theme of the Annunciation, the celebration of a miraculous pregnancy in a virgin which was to bring the hope of eternal life to sinful mankind, could find its reflection in the new growth now springing, however tentatively, in the world of nature. Poets, eager to seize on opportune links and correspondences in imaginatively interpreting their world, grasped the literary possibilities presented by the season of Easter and the Annunciation by reinforcing with natural imagery the important devotional and doctrinal messages of hope.

The conventional language and imagery of secular spring- and love-poetry were pressed into service to celebrate Mary's spotless excellence and loving obedience in accepting her role as Mother of God, and Christ's overflowing love in giving Himself for all mankind. One Middle English Easter poem opens with lines which could introduce any lyric celebrating earthly love, before settling into a narrative of the Crucifixion: 'Spring has come and winter has gone; daylight begins to lengthen, and all these birds rejoice in song. So strongly does sorrow bind me, despite the joy felt in the world, for the sake of a young nobleman who is very gracious with his hand.' The 'young nobleman' is Christ, spoken of as a romantic hero with whom it would be possible to fall in love in springtime.

The adaptation of the spring love-song for religious use depended upon the church's willingness to interpret parts of the Bible allegorically, as an expression of love between Christ and the human soul, or Christ and the church. Particularly influential on both religious and love poetry was the Old Testament 'Song of Solomon', an intense love-poem using garden imagery and settings. The allegorical tradition joined forces with medieval developments in devotional thinking, notably an emerging willingness to see human family and erotic affections not as a distraction to be renounced, as the early ascetics thought, but as a rung on the ladder to Divine love and as a fitting way of expressing mortals' longing for God:

> Now that I see blossom coming out and have heard a bird's song, in my heart there has sprung up a sweet yearning caused by a new love which is so sweet and true that it makes my heart joyous. I know with certainty that my life and my happiness, too, are completely dependent upon it. I sing of Jesus Christ, who is so handsome and noble, the sweetest of all creatures; truly, I ought to be his own . . .

In this fifteenth-century Flemish illustration of the
Annunciation, the archangel Gabriel is depicted with the good
looks of a handsome nobleman, while Mary appears as a
modest, well-born young woman. The teeming life of the
border of the painting reflects the theme of new birth

A variety of spring agricultural activities: in the foreground
wattles are being cut and plaited into fences; in the
middle ground, trees are being tended; in the distance,
fields are being ploughed

The language of courtly love, that aristocratic preoccupation so much
associated with spring, enables the Virgin Mary to be presented as the
archetypal beloved, sometimes in a spring setting, sometimes compared
favourably with the natural beauties of spring.

The high flights of courtly love and devotional imagery were a far cry
from the world of the medieval peasant, who could be forgiven for
regarding the arrival of spring with mixed feelings. On the one hand it

meant more daylight hours, relief from the double deprivation of late winter's shortages and the Lenten penitential fast, the prospect of warmer weather, and less time spent inside the stuffy and smoky houses where chimneys were few and windows small, often covered only with rudimentary shutters. On the other hand, it also brought the beginning of a season of very hard work in the fields; the period of plenty did not come immediately or without effort. Not only were there the great common fields of the village to be tilled, but much work had to be done for the lord of the manor on his lands. Only when all these commitments had been fulfilled could the peasant turn his attention to his own little garden in which many crops and plants were grown to supplement and add variety to his family diet: domestic vegetables such as cabbages, leeks, onions, beans and peas, and fruit: apples, pears, cherries and nuts.

The winter days had provided an opportunity for repairing tools. New ploughshares had been forged in the village smithy, knives and axes sharpened and handles on scythes and bill-hooks replaced. Corn and oats, carefully hoarded over the winter, were now used to feed the draught animals, building up the strength they would need to till the heavy soil when ploughing began in March. In Mediterranean countries a light scratch-plough could be used because the topsoil was thin and dry, but this was no use in the sticky clay of northern Europe, where the early middle ages saw the introduction of a heavy wheeled plough; the wheels of this machine could bear part of its weight, thus sparing to an extent the backs of the animals pulling it, usually horses or oxen.

Throughout the middle ages, returns on seed-corn were much lower than those expected by farmers today, with productivity varying depending on the availability of fertilizer and on the amount of work which could be carried out on the soil. All available animal manure had been carefully husbanded throughout the winter, and as spring approached it was spread on the fields. Straw used in the cow sheds was saved, mixed with earth, carted laboriously to the fields and ploughed in. An alternative and very good fertilizer, where available, was marl, a chalky earth; carting and spreading marl was a peasant activity frequently referred to in manorial accounts. Even the droppings of the pigeons and doves populating the numerous dovecotes in the landscape were valued as fertilizer.

The crops to be grown depended on the climate and the area involved.

By the later middle ages, many of the great agricultural areas of Europe were cultivated on a threefold rotation system designed to prevent exhaustion of the soil. One third of the land was left fallow, one third sown with a crop such as winter wheat and one third with spring corn, perhaps wheat or barley. Broadly speaking, in the spring the crops used primarily for horse fodder and drink grains, such as oats and barley, were widely sown, while in autumn it was the bread grains, rye and wheat. Oats were crucial for feeding draught animals and were grown as far south as possible, although they were not very tolerant of the summer heat of the Mediterranean, where horses might have to be fed barley. Barley, being tolerant of climate, was widely grown even as far north as Scandinavia. It was used as a base for both porridge and bread; it would also be fermented to make ale. Rye and millet were other common crops; millet suited light soils and was especially grown in the Pyrenees, south-west France and northern Italy.

March, as so many illustrations in Books of Hours show, was the month for the first ploughing, followed by harrowing, then by the sowing of the spring corn crop with seed-corn carefully saved over the winter. The experience of successive generations of peasants had developed an efficient way of distributing seed: a box called a 'seed lip' was hung around the sower's neck and from it he scattered handfuls of seeds. A description in one Book of Husbandry suggests a sort of rolling gait – when the right foot was in front a handful of seeds was taken from the seed lip, when the left foot was in front the seed was scattered. Alternatively, an apron could be used to carry the seeds. Peas and beans were sown differently, frequently by women, and back-breaking it must have been to make the individual holes with a pointed stick and drop seeds into them one by one. Legumes were an important part of medieval food crops; medieval people were in a very literal sense 'full of beans'!

The greatest danger to the vital crops at this early stage of the year was that birds would eat the seed. Walter of Henley, in his *Book of Husbandry* written in the late thirteenth century, warns against the 'crows, doves and other birds' which would eat the seed as it was scattered. In order to cover the seed and thus protect it, harrowing was carried out again immediately after sowing. 'Things grafted or planted, the greatest and least, defend against tempest, the bird and the beast' was the advice offered by one piece

The three main crop-sowing activities are pictured here: in the background two horses draw a heavy wheeled plough; in the middle a man casts seeds carried in his apron; in the foreground a harrow is used to cover the seed

of sixteenth-century doggerel. The lord of the manor would own a substantial harrow with a toothed underside; on poorer plots peasants might have to make do with a bush harrow, which was simply, as its name suggests, a bush dragged across the ground. Medieval illustrations show children busy following the harrow, hurling stones to fend off the crowds of greedy birds. One French illustration shows a man behind the harrow with

Vines had to be pruned and staked in early spring. Later in the
season, from the vantage-point of the wooden tower, men
could keep watch over the ripening grapes

his bow and arrow, deterring the predators and acquiring a welcome
addition for his table at the same time. More commonly, birds for the table
were trapped or caught in nets.

The third of the land which lay fallow did not produce crops, but it
might support a few sheep; Walter of Henley suggests two per acre. Even
when lying fallow, however, the land had to be worked, and in April it
would be given the first of three seasonal ploughings, this one to break up
the hard, frozen ground.

Ploughing, sowing and harrowing were the first priorities for the early

These plump birds have clearly been bred for domestic
consumption and offer no resistance to the fowler's net. A
further source of food is being exploited by the man fishing in
the moat

spring. Once they had been completed other tasks awaited the peasants,
on their own land, on the communal land and on their lords' lands; these
varied from region to region, but nearly everywhere there were ditches to
be cleared, broken banks to be rebuilt and hedges and fences in need of
attention. Manorial account rolls, which might appear on the surface to be
unexciting documents, in fact provide a vivid picture of seasonal rural life.
They show the costs of making and repairing tools, of keeping animals, of
repairing the mills and the cowsheds and other farm buildings – and
miscellaneous expenses such as twopence paid to the man who caught

sixteen moles in a meadow belonging to the bishop of Winchester. They also describe customary work carried out by villeins on the estates. It was very varied and at this time of year might include carting manure, roofing ewe-houses, making hurdles for the sheepfold, cleaning the mill-pond, carting timber to the mill, gathering and transporting thorns and brambles for making enclosures, carrying firewood to the manor house, making hurdles for eel-beds, washing and shearing sheep – and of course much ploughing and harrowing. On some manors reference is made to constructing new buildings with timber or with wattle and daub; for this timber had to be cut and implements made or repaired. The burdens of these obligations varied, but peasants would often spend a substantial part of each week at the busiest seasons working for their lord.

Still, in the longer days of spring and summer, many peasants completed their day's work for their lord long before dusk and were then free to tend their own houses and gardens or crofts. After a hard winter the huts might need repair: the peasant was often entitled to some of his lord's timber for this purpose, though many huts were constructed mainly of wattle and daub. Crops could be grown in the croft or little enclosure around the peasant dwelling: that of the poor widow in Chaucer's 'Nun's Priest's Tale' is described as a yard enclosed by palings and a dry ditch.

Thomas Tusser, the sixteenth-century agricultural theorist and versifier, advised: 'In March and in April, from morning to night,/in sowing and setting, good housewives delight:/To have in a garden or other like plot,/to turn up their house and to furnish their pot.' These crops provided a useful supplement to the standard diet of bread and pottage – essentially a watery stock to which vegetables could be added – and provided much-needed variety. Whereas what was grown on the village common fields depended on the communal decision, families were free to choose what they planted on their own plots.

Thomas Tusser's rhyming advice for March praised leeks: 'Now leeks are in season, for pottage full good,/and spareth the milch cow and purgeth the blood./These having with peas for pottage in Lent,/thou sparest both oatmeal and bread to be spent.' Peas and beans might also be grown on the common fields to provide fodder for animals as well as humans: even bread could be made of beans if necessary. Onions were praised by one commentator in the early sixteenth century: 'They stir appetite to meat

The building of a manor house, a scene taken from a treatise on agriculture. The tools and techniques of the builders are clearly depicted. In the background a formal garden has been laid out

and put away lothsomeness and loose the belly, they quicken sight and being eaten in great abundance with meat, they cause one to sleep soundly.' Few peasants would be in a position to eat them in great abundance with meat, but they were a popular village crop. Herbs too were widely grown, including parsley, garlic and mustard. Most peasants would also have a pig which could be fed on scraps and, in the autumn, on acorns

A flock of sheep is being driven out to pasture from their winter
quarters past a cow which is being milked. In the background
a woman is churning butter

and other nuts. A piece of pork or bacon was the most common form in which many medieval men and women tasted meat. Chaucer's poor widow in 'The Nun's Priest's Tale' kept three sows, three cows and a sheep called Molly; and the old woman's diet consisted mostly of milk and black bread, augmented by some broiled bacon and an egg or two. A further glimpse of the diet of many medieval people is given by a character in William Langland's fourteenth-century poem *Piers Plowman*:

> I haven't a penny to buy pullets, geese or pigs, but only two fresh cheeses, a little curds and cream, an oat-cake, and two loaves made of beans and bran which I baked for my children. And moreover, I swear by my soul that I haven't any salt bacon or, good heavens, even an egg to make eggs-and-bacon with! But I've got some parsley, some leeks and plenty of greens, and a cow and calf, and a draught mare to cart my dung in the fields. . .

Beyond the village, spring was also welcomed by richer sections of the community. Travelling became much easier, and many manorial lords took the opportunity of moving from one of their houses to another, elsewhere in the country, for it was often easier for the lord and his family to travel round their estates than it was to cart produce to their principal manor. Many roads – hardly more than tracks in modern terms – would become almost impassable in winter, and in spring the numbers of travellers on the road swelled. The lords would travel on horseback, with their household possessions carried on carts, normally sent on ahead of the main party, since the carts could travel only very slowly. Great ladies and the elderly and infirm were often carried in horse-litters. Many travellers just walked, perhaps accompanied by a heavily laden donkey. Travelling in whatever fashion was at any time a difficult and uncertain business: for example, the maintenance of many roads depended on the goodwill of the landowners. In the fifteenth century, King Charles VI of France described roads outside Paris as 'much injured, damaged, or decayed and otherwise hindered, by ravines of water and great stones, by hedges, brambles and many other trees.' However, because so much of the travelling was done by the great landowners themselves, and the clergy, it was in their interest to ensure that at least the main highways remained passable. Petitions were

A lady in a partially enclosed waggon travels along a stony
highway. In this fifteenth-century Flemish illustration
of an allegorical French work, she represents
the soul on its rough journey through life

frequently directed to parliament for the roads to be repaired, although not
always with much effect; indeed, the 1339 English parliament was itself
delayed because the prelates and lords were so troubled by bad weather that
they could not arrive in time.

The famous opening lines of Chaucer's prologue to *The Canterbury Tales*
remind us that spring was the season when devotional as well as domestic
travel came into medieval people's minds: 'When April has penetrated
March's drought to the root with its sweet showers . . . people long to go on

A mixed group of travellers showing laymen and
churchmen perhaps on pilgrimage

pilgrimages, and palmers long to visit foreign shores and distant shrines,
famous all over the world.' The great medieval pilgrimage sites of Europe
were Rome, the shrine of St James at Compostella, the relics of the Three
Kings at Cologne and Becket's tomb at Canterbury, but there were many
sites of national or local importance which attracted substantial numbers
of travellers. Such journeys could be dangerous: a letter from Agnes Paston
in East Anglia in the mid-fifteenth century describes the capture of two
pilgrims by coastal pillagers. Fortunately in this case, the pillagers were

Spectators on the river banks enjoy scenes of water-tilting

A priest makes the sign of the cross with ashes on the heads of
his congregation on Ash Wednesday at the beginning of Lent

Rustics, with may branches in their headgear, celebrate May
Day by dancing to the music of the bagpipes

clearly either God-fearing or well aware of the penalties incurred by those
who attacked pilgrims, for on discovering that the travellers were on
pilgrimage they released them unharmed.

Even for those who could not go on pilgrimages, spring was not just a
time for work; it was also a time of feasts and festivals, both religious and
secular, some of them, indeed, mingling pagan and agricultural customs
with Christian celebrations. In a number of French villages, the first
Sunday in Lent was the occasion for the dance of the Brandon; men and
women carrying candles went into the fields, sang liturgical songs, danced
and uttered prayers against pests harmful to vegetation. Lent, the season of
fasting, came at the appropriate time of the year in practical terms, when
the previous winter's crops were already in short supply. However, before
the weeks of abstinence began, Shrove Tuesday was a day for children's
sports, some of them cruel by today's standards; as the antiquarian Stow
describes, '[in London] the school boys do bring cocks of the game to their
master and all the forenoon delight themselves in cockfighting: after
dinner, all the youths go into the fields to play at the ball.' Stow continues
his description by relating that at Easter, young men also fight mock
battles on the water. A shield, attached to a pole in the middle of the
stream, is to be charged by a youth in a boat moving downstream with the
tide. The young man must try to break his lance against the shield without
falling into the water: if he does fall in, two accompanying boats are there
to rescue him.

Celebrating the spring

Easter was the first great church festival of the year, a movable feast on the borders between late winter and early spring. Itself a solemn, if joyful, occasion, it was followed by revelry: in England young people let off steam during the Hockdays, the Monday and Tuesday after Easter. On Hock Monday the women of the village could seize the men and hold them to ransom; on the following day it was the turn of the men to imprison the women. Much enjoyment and much disorder resulted, and not surprisingly attempts were made to check them. In 1409 the London authorities issued a prohibition pronouncing that 'No person in the city of London . . . shall take hold of or constrain any person of whatsoever estate or condition he may be, within house or without . . . ' Church authorities also tried to curb what they considered to be pagan festivals; ironically, ecclesiastical prohibitions tell us a great deal about these forbidden celebrations, for example May Day, an occasion of special rejoicing in honour of the coming of spring when men and women walked out in the meadows and woods and praised the beauties of flowers and nature, returning to village or town celebrations. In Worcester, the bishop tried to prevent the traditional May Day festivities in which a village girl was chosen as Queen of the May to be crowned with a garland of flowers.

It was not just the supposed pagan elements in these activities that aroused the opposition of the church, but also the threat of public disorder, which might end in injury to participants. Many a game of football (then a fairly brutal sport) played in the churchyard on holidays resulted in bloodshed. At a conference held by the French and English in Calais in 1439, intended to discuss peace terms for the ending of the Hundred Years' War, several of the commissioners were unable to attend one of the meetings, because they had been injured while playing football!

March, April and May were busy but enjoyable months. If the weather was not too unfavourable, it was hoped that the intensive labour of springtime would result in good harvests later in the year. There was much to look forward to and much to keep people constructively occupied in the attempt to ensure that the year's activities would be profitable.

SUMMER

According to the *Secretum Secretorum*, summer began when the sun entered the sign of Cancer in mid-June, and lasted until the sun entered Libra in mid-September. The longer daylight hours and warmer weather brought many welcome changes: there is 'tranquillity in the sea, clearness in the air, grains dry and ripen, serpents come forth, poisons are dispersed and bodily virtues are strengthened.' Summer is compared to a married woman at her peak of physical perfection. Medieval physiology saw pitfalls even in so perfect a season, however; the disruptive humour choler, hot and dry, was the dominant bodily influence in summer, and so excessive hot food and drink, and food likely to cause digestive upsets, were to be avoided. Cool, moist foods like veal dressed with vinegar, cucumber, chicken, pottages based on barley, and sharp fruits like apples and pomegranates were recommended. Anything heating, such as lovemaking and baths, should be avoided. Much of the advice is in fact purely practical, based on what foods become available in summer. The *Secretum Secretorum* concludes its recommendations with this venerable principle: 'in the same way through all the seasons of the year one must cure contraries with contraries.'

Summer's role was above all to ripen crops and fruit. Anxiety about the possibility of a poor summer was never far away, for a poor summer meant a thin winter. The early fifteenth-century poet Thomas Hoccleve wrote a punning *balade* and roundel to Sir Henry Somer ('Summer'), a begging-poem asking him to be generous with Christmas gifts to his servants (Hoccleve and his cronies), as if he were the summer sun being entreated to look kindly on the earth and cause 'all fruit to wax and spring'. Like anxious farmers in summer, Hoccleve and his colleagues dread bad weather: 'we are out of our minds with the fear of storms.' But Sir Henry Somer/Summer is also addressed in terms expressing a more general delight in the hot season: 'Summer, you who ripen man's sustenance with the wholesome heat of the sun's warmth, should be blessed by all manner of men. May your friendly demeanour, and your attractive, cheerful and happy appearance be ever thanked!' The fruitful richness of the later part of summer bordering on autumn was a cause of rejoicing, whether or not it had been preceded by deprivation, as celebrated in the Middle English romance *King Alexander*: 'At harvest-time it is very pleasant; pears and apples hang on the boughs. The hayward cheerfully blows his horn, the corn is ripe in every field, and the grapes hang on the vine.' Joy in summer's productivity could even be given a religious significance; as the ninth-century theologian Hrabanus Maurus had put it, 'summer indeed is the foreshadowing of future rejoicing, and it expresses the heat of [Divine] love . . . Summer signifies the blessedness to come . . .'

Traditional Biblical imagery encouraged an allegorical or symbolic interpretation of summer as the time of spiritual harvest; in the fourteenth-century vision-poem *Pearl*, the narrator, mourning his lost 'pearl', his dead baby daughter, swoons and dreams in a grassy garden 'in August, at a high festival, when the corn is cut with sharp scythes'. This bereaved father has to learn the hard way to rejoice (as a Christian should) in his lost child's salvation, for what was sown in corruption will be raised incorruptible, a spiritual harvest of which the earthly harvest is but a faint shadow. Still, on the human level there remains a painful contrast between the man's loss and the abundance of the harvest landscape.

The harvest itself was the main event of summer. It had an 'official' beginning at Lammas, on 1 August, though for practical reasons this marked a symbolic rather than an actual start. 'Lammas', from the Anglo-Saxon word meaning 'Loaf-mass', was the occasion when bread made from the first-fruits of the new harvest was blessed in church: an occasion much looked forward to by the poorer peasants. In the fourteenth-century poem *Piers Plowman*, the virtuous ploughman of that name talks of keeping hunger at bay with parsley, leeks, green vegetables and the produce of his cow and calf until Lammas, when his exhausted stores of grain can be replenished: 'By this sustenance we can live until Lammas, and by that time I intend to have a harvest in my field; then I'll be able to prepare your dinner as I'd really like to.'

The long summer days were the medieval peasant's busiest time. Labours of the Months sequences often illustrate summer with pictures of hay-mowing, weeding and fruit-gathering; on the Continent, where the

These fifteenth-century Italian fruit-pickers look
mischievous but their possession of a trough may
indicate that their activity is legitimate

harvest came earlier, reaping and threshing are common for July and
August. The main crops might vary from one area of Europe to another but
the long days of work were the same whether the crops were grain, grapes
or olives, for crops had to be gathered in from the peasants' own little plots,
from the communal village strips and from the lord's demesne lands. It was
the lord's land which took priority: throughout the summer months, from
Midsummer to Michaelmas, not only did the peasants have to fulfil
additional days of labour on their lord's land as part of their commitments,
but they were also expected to do 'boon days'. These were days of labour,
theoretically given out of good will, when a peasant would turn up with all
the members of his family, men and women (except the housewife), to
gather in the crops. In return a meal and ale would be provided by the lord.
Such days could not be fixed long in advance: the steward of the manor or
his officials would decree them when the weather was suitable, calling on
peasants to appear on the next day for a 'boon'.

The first crop to be cut in the summer was the hay. Much of it was of
poor quality; the best was that grown in water meadows near rivers likely to

A peasant couple working together to bring in the harvest,
perhaps from their section of one of the large communal fields.
The village church can be seen in the background

flood during the winter and deposit rich silt on the land. The hay was cut at
the rate of about one acre per person per day, using long scythes with
blades set almost at right angles to the handle. Men and women would
work in groups, divided around the large fields, supervised by the village
reeve, an overseer elected by the peasants. The men cut the hay; the girls
and women raked and turned it. Blades would blunt or be broken,
requiring rapid mending by a man sitting in the corner of the field doing
running repairs with a whetstone. The most festive and pleasant of these
days of communal activity were those designated as 'wet boons' when the
manor servants would provide ale for the workers, carried to them at their
work so that they could refresh themselves as often as they liked. Food too
was provided by the lord for the midday meal: perhaps a finer bread than
many of the peasants normally ate, together with hunks of cheese.

The long day was ended at dusk by the blowing of the hayward's horn.
The workers then went to the manor house, or at least to one of its
outhouses, for a good meal as a reward for their boon labours. For the
poorer villagers this meal would be a rare treat, with roast meat in addition
to the customary pease pottage, cheese and ale. On some manors villagers
were allowed to claim for themselves as much hay as they could carry on
their scythe. Greedy men tried to overload their tools and then lost their
entire load when they failed to carry it successfully from the field.

Work was unrelenting at this period: once the hay was in, the wheat
needed to be weeded, the fallow strips needed their second ploughing and
thistles had to be uprooted. In England it was considered unlucky to uproot

A welcome interruption to a hard day's work in the fields; two peasants refresh themselves. Cornflowers and poppies can be clearly seen amongst the corn. On the far bank of the river a cartload of sheaves is being taken to the barn

Skill and care were needed in the binding of all sheaves, not just
the final ceremonial one for 'Harvest Home'. Here a French
peasant concentrates intently on his task.
Opposite: The harvest in progress

thistles before 24 June, St John's Day; country legend claimed that thistles uprooted before then would multiply threefold. Other troublesome weeds – dock, marigolds, chicory, fennel, speargrass – had to be cleared from the crops. Meanwhile women gathered hemp and flax, some of which might be grown in their own little plots. Hemp was uprooted, not cut, then laid in a stream where the fleshy part was rubbed away and beaten to separate the fibres. (People who fouled public water with hemp were unpopular.) The hemp was hung up to dry, after which it would be spun on a spindle to make thread or rope.

Once the hay was in, the reaping of grain crops and vetches began. Peas, beans, barley and oats were cut with scythes, often by teams of men and women, four to cut and one to bind. When harvesting grains, reapers worked in groups along the ploughing ridges, some cutting and others following behind to bind and stack the sheaves, from time to time exchanging activities to rest different sets of muscles. Sheaves, round or long, were kept small to be easily carried. Wheat was cut with a sickle, high up on the stalk near to the head; the straw was left standing, either being cut later to feed the cattle or, if fodder was plentiful, being ploughed back in and left to rot as valuable enrichment of the soil. Once the fields were bare of crops, the poor were allowed to come and glean; after that, animals would be allowed to wander over them, picking up any food they could.

For the harvesters themselves, the end of the harvest was festive. To mark it, various games and ceremonies evolved, such as racing to finish the last ridge, or leaving a special section of corn to be ceremonially cut at the end, or putting the last sheaf, decorated or plaited, on top of the last hay-wagon, the hock-cart, on its way to the barn. It was customary for the lord to give a harvest supper to celebrate the successful completion of the work.

It was expensive to provide meals for the harvesters. This consideration, together with the increasing resentment shown by those bound to perform labour services, led, as the middle ages progressed, to the commutation of labour services for cash payments and an increased use of paid casual labour instead. One major problem was that peasants forced to work lacked motivation; and they were often suspected of stealing corn. A feeling of resentment against the system perhaps accounts for the popularity in many parts of Europe of the story of St Zita, a servant girl who stole corn from her

In the foreground a man rakes the crop together. In the
background other villagers hoist the sheaves into the barn

master to feed the poor. When the manorial officials came to investigate
the loss of corn, the corn barrel was found to have been miraculously
refilled!

Accounts kept by manorial officials give an idea of how hard peasants
laboured, and of the range of their summer tasks. At one southern English
manor in the fourteenth century, thirty-nine customary tenants who held
their plots by virtue of their service carried out 2,847 different tasks
between the feast of the Annunciation and Lammas. The main ones
included weeding the corn, ploughing and harrowing for the barley to be
sown in the autumn, washing and shearing sheep, mowing and lifting hay
and gathering twigs. Other miscellaneous duties included carrying thorns
and brambles for enclosing the compound, carrying firewood, carting
wool, and shepherding. Thomas Tusser's *Five Hundred Points of Good
Husbandry* suggests various maintenance tasks and preparatory activities as
appropriate for the summer months. Early ploughing should be done in
June, outbuildings and barns should be repaired and made watertight, carts
should be mended, troublesome bushes and brambles should be rooted out
and new hop-plots should be dug. Hops became increasingly important as
beer slowly grew in popularity against the native unhopped ale made from
malted grain.

In many parts of Europe, June was also the month for shearing sheep.
The main culling of the flock would have been carried out in May, when
the lambs were weaned. From now until early September the ewes would
provide valuable milk, more prized than that of cows and popular for
cheese-making. Sheep selected for disposal were shorn early, put out to
pasture to be fattened and then sold about midsummer when mutton was
in season. Richer peasants might have a small flock of sheep of their own;
the poorer were perhaps lucky to have a single one.

In June, before Midsummer's Day, the feast of St John, the sheep would
be washed in a pond or a stream, preferably in running water because of the
vast amount of filth their skins could hold. They were then shorn. In the
great sheep-rearing areas, shearing the lord's sheep was the main boon
work of the summer and was carried out by both men and women. A small
pair of shears could be found among most peasants' tools. Wool was either
sold or spun to provide cloth for the family. It might well provide a vital
cash crop, for not even the most industrious peasant family could be

The technique of sheep-shearing remained constant for centuries. Here two wriggling sheep are being shorn; on the left one waits whilst on the right is a sheep newly-shorn

entirely self-sufficient. For those involved in the sheep clipping, the shearing supper was as great an event as the harvest supper later in the year.

Among other produce harvested in the summer was honey. Beehives were a common sight in the landscape of medieval Europe and honey was the chief source of sweetness for rich and poor alike, for cooking, for sweetening wine and for making mead. Honey was also considered valuable by physicians and apothecaries, and beeswax was used in making candles for the wealthy and for ointments, perhaps mixed with a sweet-smelling floral essence such as violet. The keeping of hives was not just the prerogative of the great lords; some smallholders had their own hives and might expect to pay part of their rent in honey or wax. Careful keepers would expect each hive to produce about nine litres of honey a year, as well as wax.

The swarming of the bees normally took place in June or July. Each hive of bees was expected to produce two swarms a year, with early swarms particularly desirable: according to an old proverb, 'a swarm in May is worth a load of hay'. Thomas Tusser suggested that between the hours of ten and three, when a swarming might occur, the hives should be watched. This was considered a suitable task for a small child who could at the same time occupy itself by spinning, knitting or sewing. Swarming was a noisy process, not because of the fierce humming of the bees, but because of the country practice of beating kettles or tin pans and clapping and whistling by those following the swarm. The resulting clamour served as a

Salt making was a hot and exhausting job. Here, two men work
to keep the furnace of the boiling-house fuelled, while their
companions stir the hot saline solution

A man, possibly in protective head-gear, beats a pan as the
swarming bees settle. Bees were classified not as insects, but as
birds, by many medieval naturalists

warning to neighbours that the swarm was taking place and was regarded as
a claim on the swarm wherever it settled: it was also widely believed that
the noise would help the bees to settle. When the bees landed they could
be caught on a sheet on which stood a wicker or wooden hive smeared with
honey or cream to attract them. At night the entrance to the hive would
be blocked up, except for a couple of bee holes. The ideal site for a hive was
raised above ground level, near grass and flowers. It had to be protected
from the winds from the north and north-east, and from rain, as well as
from vermin and farm animals.

Those involved in the vital industry of salt-making were also actively
occupied during the summer months. Along the French Atlantic coast
and on the beaches of north Spain and Portugal salt was prepared from sea-
water. Huge dishes were filled with salt water which was evaporated by the
hot sun. Although the resulting salt was full of impurities, it was popular
for preserving because it penetrated meat thoroughly and had a palatable
sweet–sharp taste. In England the element 'wich' in place-names
frequently denotes places where salt was made. Around Droitwich, for
example, huge brine pits were dug, perhaps thirty feet deep, down to a

layer through which brine seeped from underground springs. Between June and December, when the brine was strongest and the pits were least likely to flood, bucketfuls of brine were winched up. Both near these pits and on the coast, boiling-houses were used to obtain the salt from brine. These timber huts contained enormous pans of lead, standing on bricks over grates, into which the buckets of brine were tipped. The salt-fires ate up vast quantities of fuel, for a fierce heat was needed. A quick preliminary boiling removed foreign bodies; a slower boiling followed to evaporate the water. The residue was drawn out with long wooden rakes and dried in conical baskets. Two sorts of salt could be produced: the coarse-grained version most suitable for preserving meat was produced by boiling the brine for long periods, while fine table salts were produced by quick boiling. Families which could afford it purchased both preserving salt and table salt.

Summer, despite the hard labour of the harvest, offered opportunities for outdoor diversions of many kinds. The Hungarian historian Walter Endrei, contrasting modern and medieval attitudes to games, observes that 'it must rather sadly be admitted that nowadays adults hardly ever play outdoor games. The bulk of outdoor games have become the privilege of children and some have become transformed into simple exercises, and not infrequently into competitive sport.' He also notes the social function of medieval outdoor games in bringing people of different classes together in a way inconceivable with indoor games. To illustrate this he quotes a description in a fifteenth-century chronicle of Zürich: 'Tables stand under the lime trees, chess and draughts boards upon them . . . there is also a bowling alley and other games [including sporting competitions]. Nobles and citizens go on the mountains and under the lime trees, and shoot at the butts with crossbows.' The sixteenth-century English antiquary John Stow describes a similar social 'levelling' in the summer games of medieval London youth, though this is manifest among the spectators rather than the participants, when the aldermen, fathers and city magnates ride to the fields to watch the boys playing ball games. Other diversions take place: 'On holidays all the summer the boys play at archery practice, running, jumping, wrestling, putting the stone, sending missiles attached with thongs [slingshots or catapults?] beyond a mark, and duelling with bucklers. The girls Cytherea leads in dancing until moonrise, and the earth is beaten with the lively foot.'

Garden games such as bowls provided ideal opportunities for
young aristocrats to spend time in each other's company

Children teach each other to swim. One is making good
progress, but a younger child shivers as he stands uncertainly
in the shallower water

Children's summer games could be solitary or communal, and
occasionally rather cruel. The French poet and chronicler Froissart
derived great amusement as a child from capturing butterflies and tying
threads to them so that they had to fly where he wished. Rather less
objectionably, he liked floating things down the local brook, blowing
soap-bubbles and playing a wide variety of communal games with
intriguing names, many of which remain unidentified. Naughtiness found
ready outlets in the numerous summer opportunities for juvenile petty
theft of crops or, to put it more kindly, scrumping. The fifteenth-century
monk of Bury St Edmunds, John Lydgate, who in his adulthood became a
very dignified and sententious poet, gives us a welcome glimpse of his less
stuffy childhood in this description of stealing fruit: 'I ran into gardens,
where I stole apples; I spared neither hedge nor wall in gathering fruit. I
was more ready to pick grapes from other people's vines than to say Matins
. . . I put all my five wits to wasteful use, preferring to count cherry-stones
rather than go to church or listen to the holy bell.' (He seems to be
referring to a game in which cherry-stones were used either as counters or
as jacks.) The late medieval poet Alexander Barclay hints in one of his
Eclogues at the successful fruit-stealing which can be deduced from the

Flemish guildsmen, wearing the characteristic dress of their
guild, display their skills in shooting with cross-bows. In the
middle of the picture an attendant cranks up a bow

cheerfulness of small boys in summer: 'Look in the streets, behold the little
boys, How in fruit-season for joy they sing and hop.'

Less energetic diversions and more adult pleasures could be found
outdoors in summer in gardens and orchards. Gardens came in many
different kinds: the kitchen garden, the herber or grassy plot, and the
manorial pleasure garden; and orchards, too, were much valued. Summer

was a time for high-born women to wander in their gardens, beautifully kept for recreational purposes. A German Dominican friar, Albertus Magnus, writing in about 1250, describes pleasure gardens designed, not for fruitfulness, but to delight the senses of sight and smell. Albertus was a much-travelled man of noble birth who was clearly familiar with the gardens he described. He stresses the health-giving value of fresh air in a pleasant environment, and sets down instructions for obtaining a good lawn, which should be surrounded by sweet-smelling herbs such as rue, sage and basil as well as by flowers such as violets, columbines, lilies, roses and irises. The ideal pleasure garden, Albertus claims, needed also to have trees or vines trained to ensure shade as well as sunshine: '. . . let them be sweet trees with perfumed flowers such as pears, apples, cypresses'. If possible, a clear fountain of water should also be provided. Such pleasure gardens are frequently depicted in lavishly illustrated medieval manuscripts, both in secular contexts, for example in pictures of lovers in gardens, and in devotional images: the Virgin and Child are painted in exterior settings, as well as against interior backdrops. Netherlandish paintings of the fifteenth century which depict domestic interiors with precision often also show a distant garden through a window. King James I of Scotland, held captive in Windsor Castle in the early fifteenth century, described the garden he could see from his prison.

Gardens were the setting for gentle, flirtatious games and much love-play in the middle ages, if even a fraction of the fictionalized wooings presented in lyrics and romances bears any relation to fact. Lovers are very often portrayed in green and flowery gardens; although the most famous literary examples (such as the thirteenth-century French love-allegory *The Romance of the Rose*) tend to be set in spring, particularly May, rather than summer, in visual illustrations it is very hard to draw the line between the two seasons, a difficulty increased by the artists' cheerful indifference to realism in the flowering-times of plants, a casualness which accords very oddly with their meticulous depictions of individual flowers.

'Social' games involving mild horseplay, like the popular blind-man's-buff, could lead to further dalliance in alfresco settings. The *carole* or ring-dance, as depicted in *The Romance of the Rose*, for example, could be danced in a garden, and with its leisurely pace and alternating periods of standing still and holding hands in a ring with periods of moving round in a

One of the most famous medieval love-gardens is described in
the thirteenth-century allegorical poem, *The Romance of the
Rose*. It was frequently richly illustrated

A lively game of blind-man's-buff amongst
young aristocrats in a garden

circle, it offered an ideal opportunity for flirtation. Picnics provided other
occasions for dalliance. An idealized picture of a leisurely summer picnic
for two appears in a fourteenth-century poem by Philippe de Vitry:

> Under the green leaves, on the soft turf beside a chattering brook
> with a clear spring near at hand, I found a rustic hut set up. Gontier
> and Dame Helen were dining there, on fresh cheese, milk, butter,
> cheesecake, cream, curds, apples, nuts, plums, pears; they had garlic
> and onions and crushed shallots, on crusty black bread with coarse
> salt to give them a thirst. They drank from the jug and the birds made
> music to cheer the hearts of both lover and lass, who next exchanged
> their loving kisses on mouth and nose, the smooth face and the
> bearded.

Bear-hunting was particularly dangerous. Here a bear at bay
has killed at least two dogs and has grasped the huntsman's
spear in his paw to deflect it

Hunting dominated the leisure activities of the upper classes throughout
Europe in the middle ages, not merely as a sport but also as a suitable
preparation for warfare, a means of keeping men fit and trained in the
bearing of arms. Packs of hunting dogs were an integral part of noble
households, as were trained huntsmen skilled in their craft. Gaston,
Count of Foix, who wrote the most popular of the late medieval
handbooks, *Livre de Chasse*, kept, according to the chronicler Froissart, a
pack of sixteen hundred dogs. Many different types of dogs were used for
hunting; they were divided into two main sorts, the limners, trained to
stalk and seek out the quarry silently, and the speedy dogs who would
pursue it to the kill.

The great heroes of romantic fiction in the later middle ages were well
versed in hunting, Tristram or Tristan being the doyen of them all, and the
chase played an important role in many tales. In addition to the featuring
of the chase in fictional works, manuals of hunting were very popular all
over Europe in the fourteenth and fifteenth centuries. One of these, the
Modus et Ratio, describes ten principal game animals, divided into two
groups: five sweet or fawn-coloured beasts, namely the stag or hart, its
female equivalent the hind, the fallow deer, the roe deer and the hare; and
five black beasts, also described as the sour or smelly beasts, namely the

A huntsman has been sent to scout out the quarry.
Specially trained dogs known as limners often
accompanied them in their search

boar, the wild sow, the wolf, the fox and the otter. Each had its season of
greatest popularity, in winter the wild boar and the bear, and in Lent the
hare. The greatest hunts, however, were the stag hunts which took place
in the summer, when the beasts were at their finest: in France the season
ran between the two holy days dedicated to the Holy Rood, 4 May and 14
September.

A great hunt was a carefully organized occasion and an important social
event, involving extensive preparation by the lord's servants. A number of
distinct stages were prescribed. First, huntsmen accompanied by limners
began by tracking and dislodging the deer, leaving pointing branches to
mark its trail. Meanwhile the hunting party, awaiting their return,
picnicked in an attractive glade. 'In the soft summer season when all of
nature rejoices and when small birds sing . . . the place where the gathering
is, is a lovely place, delicious and hidden . . .' as the *Modus et Ratio* puts it.
The huntsmen would report their findings, and the party would set out,
posting relays of dogs as they went. At the spot where the stag had last been
seen, the dogs were unleashed to pursue the noble animal. An elaborate
code of signals blown on the curved hunting horns had been developed to
mark the progress of the hunt, combined with a variety of calls and shouts
to urge on the dogs, such as 'Cy va, cy va, cy va!', used to call the hounds

These deer are very near to being caught at bay. The hunting
party has driven them towards a strategically-placed net.
Lower: The bulk of the carcase is being loaded onto a
cart while the dogs enjoy their reward. Two huntsmen
blow a ceremonial horn-call

when any signs of the stag were seen. A stag might double back, attempt to start other animals and take to water-courses in an attempt to escape the hunting party, but finally the speed and endurance of the dogs would force it to turn and stand its ground. This was a dangerous moment because the desperate animal might kill the hounds or attack a man on his horse. The hounds surrounded the stag and bayed, thus allowing the rest of the pack a chance to catch up. 'Hallali!' was the cry used to urge the hounds to the final attack. The huntsman approached the deer cautiously to gain a protected place from which to hamstring it. Sometimes the stag would be driven by the dogs into a strategically positioned net. A single long note on the horn marked the Blowing of the Death. Then came the most ritualistic part of the stag hunt, the Quarry, the cutting up of the animal in a prescribed order. A detailed literary example occurs in the fourteenth-century English poem, *Sir Gawain and the Green Knight*. The heart, lungs, liver and windpipe were given to the hounds, while the right forefoot of the animal was presented to the most eminent person present or to the lord of the hunt. Stags have a heart bone, a piece of hard red cartilage found in the heart which was considered to have medicinal properties; it was prized and often given to a pregnant woman. When the day's hunting was over, the party would return in triumph, with the deer in a cart, for a great feast in the lord's castle.

Ladies too were involved with the hunt, less often in the chase itself than in the social gatherings before it, the meals, the wine-drinking and the ritualistic Quarry after slaying. Some women, though, did follow the chase; the daughter of King Louis XI of France followed and despatched stags and boars herself, while a late fifteenth-century poem by Jacques de Breze, *La Chasse*, portrays a hunt presided over by a woman who herself blows the death-note. Women even wrote about hunting; it features several times in the short sentimental aristocratic romances written by Marie de France in the twelfth century.

The noble author of a popular late medieval English book, *The Master of Game*, stated 'The time of the hunter is without idleness and without evil thoughts . . . hunters live in this world more joyfully than any other men. For when the hunter rises in the morning he sees a sweet and fair morn and clear weather and bright and he heareth the song of the small birds . . . and when the sun is arisen he shall see fresh dew on the small twigs and grasses.'

Froissart's description of Count Gaston of Foix suggests that hunting was indeed a healthy sport: 'I have never seen one who was so finely built, with better proportioned limbs and body or so handsome a face, cheerful and smiling. He loved dogs more than all other animals and was very fond of hunting, both in summer and winter.' Hunting was, however, to be the Count's downfall, for as Froissart subsequently related: 'On the day of his death he had spent the whole morning until noon in the pursuit of a bear, which was finally caught. By the time it had been killed and cut up, it was mid-afternoon. He asked his men where dinner had been prepared for them . . . and rode slowly into the village.' Shortly after his arrival there, the Count collapsed and died of a stroke, brought on by over-exertion in the heat of a stifling August day.

Hunting on a grand scale was restricted to the upper echelons of society. Forest beasts – the deer, the wild boar – were protected by royal edict. The king also claimed the right to take foxes, hares, rabbits, wild cats, pheasants and partridges on his demesne lands. Most lords claimed or were granted rights of free warren which gave them the right to hunt and shoot in their estates and prevented anyone else from entering their lands to do so. Despite all these prohibitions, however, it was impossible to prevent poaching by peasants. Manorial courts frequently record the punishment of men for poaching. Bones of animals found by archaeologists reveal that many wild animals, especially small ones, were eaten in the villages. Rabbits, which had been introduced into England after the Norman conquest and had quickly begun to flourish, could be snared, thus not only providing a welcome addition to the family's diet but also removing a pest which threatened the valuable crops. Court records and literary evidence suggest that poaching was not only undertaken by men desperate for food; peasants too felt the thrill of the chase, of stalking birds and animals through forbidden territory. One fourteenth-century poem, *The Parliament of the Three Ages*, begins by describing a poacher's expedition to the woods, when with a bow and a dog he stalked and killed a stag. The poet vividly conveys the man's enjoyment involved: ' . . . in the summer season when airs are soft, I went to the wood to take my luck . . . I stayed on a bank beside a brook where the grass was green and starred with flowers – primroses, periwinkles and the rich pennyroyal. The dew dappled the daisies most beautifully and also the buds, blossoms and branches while

Getting freshwater fish into a creel required skill and good co-
ordination. Away from the coast, river fish and farmed fish were
in great demand because of the large numbers of fast-days.
Lower: A countryman aims at a heron with his cross-bow. An
aristocrat might have caught his herons by the alternative
method of using a peregrine falcon

around me the soft mists began to fall. Both the cuckoo and pigeon were singing loudly.'

Poaching was not confined to dry land: fishing both legitimately and illegitimately was popular, and the warm summer nights offered an ideal opportunity. Manor houses and monasteries had fishponds, often several, which were kept stocked; and fish could be taken from the river and the sea. Fish were vital for noble and ecclesiastical households during the penitential meatless days ordered by the church, not just Fridays but Wednesdays and Saturdays as well. There were various methods of catching fish: with rods, with nets and with traps. Trapping was also widely used to catch eels. Again, despite penalties, peasants could not be prevented from poaching fish. A court roll tells of one peasant who caught a tench in the lord's pond with his hands. He claimed in his defence that his wife had been ill for more than a month and was unable to eat. When she suddenly developed a desire for a tench, her husband went to catch one for her.

Falconry was as popular as hunting and was widely pursued by women as well as men. Like hunting, falconry was a sport of kings and the aristocracy but it also spread quite far down the social scale. John Paston, son of a Norfolk gentry family in the fifteenth century, illustrated the popular enthusiasm for the sport when he wrote to his brother: 'I ask no greater return from you for all the service that I am to perform for you throughout my life than a goshawk . . . for if I do not have a hawk I shall get fat for lack of exercise.' Falconry was a more self-indulgent sport than hunting. It required a large establishment for a small return and could never be economic: at least hunting provided food for the household. Possession of birds was closely related to status. Only the king could have a gerfalcon; nobles had to hunt with peregrines, and priests and monks with the humbler sparrow-hawk. Other birds in general use were the goshawk, the lanner and the saker. The chief source of the gerfalcon, the goshawk, the peregrine and the sparrow-hawk was Scandinavia, while the lanner and the saker came from countries bordering on the Mediterranean.

Hawks had to be trained with great care and fed on good-quality meat. King John's falcons ate doves, chicken and pork. Frequently, being much prized, they were permitted to sleep indoors on perches; they were attired with little hoods, bells and tassels. Hawks were trained to swoop upon their prey (cranes, herons, partridges, hares and rabbits), kill it, and return to the owner's left wrist, which was protected by a glove. Hawking by the water-side was considered a particularly enjoyable activity and is often depicted as a pastime of heroes in romances.

The summer period contained notable occasions of both secular and sacred importance. The first of the religious feasts was Whitsun or Pentecost which marked the descent of the Holy Spirit on the Apostles. This was considered by the church the second most important ecclesiastical festival, surpassed only by Easter fifty days earlier, and was an occasion for lay people to confess their sins and take communion. The feast of Pentecost seems to have acquired an almost romantic appeal in medieval narrative; in stories of King Arthur and his knights, the Pentecostal court feast associated with the usual religious rites is very often the occasion for some significant adventure or development, such as the mystic advent of the Holy Grail. The Arthurian court of Sir Thomas Malory's *Le Morte D'Arthur* has to renew its oath of knightly conduct annually and publicly at the feast of Pentecost.

Whitsun marked the beginning of the summer church festivals. The following Sunday was Trinity Sunday, an occasion for the celebration of God in all three Persons. Then on the Thursday after Trinity Sunday came the late medieval feast of Corpus Christi, a vivid celebration of the eucharist or mass. Its popularity increased throughout the later middle ages. All over Europe a wide range of religious processions and dramatic or semi-dramatic performances took place on and after the feast. In England these developed in the late fourteenth and fifteenth centuries into the great mystery cycles, such as those of York and Chester. These spectacles were perhaps the most enjoyable aspects of the Corpus Christi festival for the less pious. For the devout, the experience could be more intense. One pious fifteenth-century Norfolk woman, Margery Kempe, was often moved to tears by such scenes: 'And when she saw the Precious Sacrament borne about the town with lights and reverence, the people kneeling on their knees, then had she many holy thoughts and meditations, and then oftentimes would she cry and roar, as though she would have burst, for the faith and trust that she had in the Precious Sacrament.'

The great secular festival of the summer was Midsummer's Day, which was the warm season's counterpart of the Yuletide pagan festival. It was

A young man carrying a falcon on his wrist

This illustration gives some idea of the variety of birds which were hunted and of the methods of hunting them. Cross-bows, spears, nets and hunting birds are all being used. Peasants also used slings and stones

A priest holds up the communion wafer at the
Elevation of the Host in the mass

also the feast of the Nativity of St John the Baptist, though more noted for its secular celebrations, the 'Midsummer ales', than for any pious observances done in honour of the saint. Bonfires were lit, as in places they also were for the summer solstice, and were ritually leapt over. Many of the customs observed on this occasion had pre-Christian origins; hence the Church's attempts to stamp out such practices. According to one thirteenth-century description: 'On St John's Eve in certain regions the boys collect bones and certain other rubbish, and burn them, and therefrom a smoke is produced on the air. They also make brands and go about the fields with the brands. Thirdly [there is] the wheel which they roll.' In London, on Midsummer Eve the well-to-do citizens set out tables with wine and invited passers-by to drink with them.

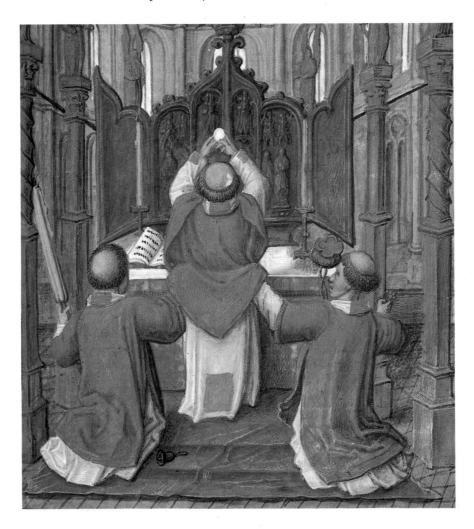

Bread of many grades was baked in wood-fired ovens.
Peasants were often obliged to use a communal village
oven provided by the lord

On the fixed feast of Lammas, 1 August, it was traditional to consecrate bread made from the first grain of the new harvest as the sacramental body of Christ in the Eucharist. For the church this was the feast of St Peter ad Vincula, but its major importance was derived from Lammas's position at the turning-point of the year of husbandry. The September and October harvest festivals celebrating the fruits of the earth, so beloved of Victorian liturgical enthusiasts, are only half the story; Lammas, which naturally associated itself with the beginning of the physical harvest, is a much stronger statement about spiritual harvests, sacramentally embodied in the communion bread.

The final major church feast day of the summer was that celebrating the Assumption of the Virgin on 15 August. The great devotion to the Virgin Mary everywhere in Europe in the later middle ages ensured the popularity of this occasion. Nowadays we can still gain some impression of the nature of this grand ecclesiastical feast of summer, if we spend it in a Mediterranean Catholic country, where processions (as in Les Saintes-Maries-de-la-Mer in France), dramas (as in Elche in Spain) and civic games (as in Siena's Palio on the day following the Assumption), provide spectacle and communal celebration on a massive scale. Less ostentatious, even comic, town and village versions of grand civic summer games evolved; nowadays festivities like the summer cheese-rolling competition of Pienza in Italy, and the chaotic Assumption Day goat-races and donkey-sweepstakes still held until a few years ago in Yssingeaux in France, represent modern descendants of medieval communal revelry in an anarchically cheerful vein appropriate to summer's lightheartedness.

AUTUMN

All over medieval Europe, in a society dominated by the rhythms of the agricultural year, autumn was a critical period during which the last of the rich crops would be harvested, freeing the land for the sowing of winter crops. In Middle English the word for autumn is in fact 'hervest' (compare our 'harvest' and the modern German word for autumn, 'Herbst'). This fruitful season began, according to the *Secretum Secretorum*, when the sun entered the sign of Libra in mid-September and lasted until mid-December, when the sun entered Capricorn. It was the period of consolidating the summer's gains, of laying in stores for the winter, and of processing the earth's produce in various ways – time-consuming, but necessary if the coming winter were not to be made miserable by deprivation.

Little of the Romantic spirit of John Keats's 'season of mists and mellow fruitfulness' is to be found in medieval literary descriptions of autumn. The *Secretum Secretorum*, rather than emphasizing the agrarian experience of autumn as a period of richness and plenty, concentrates on its characteristics as a transitional season, describing it in naturalistic terms as a time of decline and contraction, when nights lengthen, the air grows cold, north winds blow, trees lose their leaves, fruit ceases to be produced, birds migrate to hotter climates and animals seek out their dens and holes. The *Secretum* gives an impression of the season's quality with a vivid comparison to a woman of mature years, bereft of her clothes, leaving her youth behind her and hastening on to old age.

This depressing image of autumn as a woman losing her youth and beauty is melancholy in the modern emotional sense; autumn was also connected with the humour of melancholy, black bile, in the technical medieval physiological sense. Autumn, as the season of melancholy's dominance, required careful combating of the negative effects of that cold dry humour. The *Secretum Secretorum* suggests that hot moist foods like chicken, lamb and sweet grapes should be eaten and fine old wines drunk, to ward off melancholy – certainly a very pleasant-sounding remedy. Purgatives and emetics are good in autumn for clearing melancholy from the system, especially taken around noon, when the 'superfluities' or excesses of humour cause the most marked imbalances in the human frame. Overmuch exercise and lovemaking are not recommended in autumn by the *Secretum Secretorum*, but the heat and moisture of warm baths are helpful in keeping melancholy under control.

Keeping autumn's melancholy at bay was easier said than done. The early fifteenth-century poet and admirer of Chaucer, Thomas Hoccleve, wrote a poem, his 'Complaint', describing his nervous breakdown. It opens by describing his gloomy reflections, during a sleepless night in late November, linking the decline and death of the year with the inevitable decline and death of man:

> After Harvest had brought in its sheaves, and brown Michaelmastide had come and robbed the trees of their leaves, which had been green and delightful in vigour, and had dyed them a yellowish colour and cast them underfoot, that transformation affected me to the depths of my heart; for it reminded me once more that there is no stability in this world. There is nothing but change and mutability. [The world] is not going to last. Man must forego it. Death will thrust him down to the ground under his foot. That is everyone's end.

The sober message of autumn is not only that time slips away, but also that there are ordeals to be faced, whether the practical ones of surviving winter or the spiritual ones of mortality and the fate of one's soul. Linked inevitably with the hints of trials to come is the notion that one must take every possible precaution to meet their demands in advance. The association of autumn with the coming Last Judgement was traditional; in the ninth century the theologian Hrabanus Maurus explained: 'Now autumn, in which the fruits of the earth are assembled, is the time of reaping and of the vintage, and it signifies the time of the General Judgement, when every single person will receive the reward for his works.'

Hints of such urgency add depth to the powerful description of autumn's coming in the fourteenth-century English poem *Sir Gawain and the Green*

These late fourteenth-century Italian revellers may be warding
off melancholy with fine old wines, but they appear in this
manuscript as a warning against drunkenness

Knight. The hero, the Arthurian knight Sir Gawain, has agreed to accept after a year a return blow from a magical Green Knight whom he beheaded, when challenged by that knight, in a grotesque New Year's Day 'game' at Camelot. The passage of the intervening year for the apprehensive but courageous Gawain is suggested indirectly in a very beautiful description of the passage of the seasons, culminating in his departure from Arthur's court in autumn on All Souls' Day (2 November) to meet his fate:

> But then Harvest [Autumn] hastens and immediately puts heart into [the crops] and orders them to ripen fully; with drought he causes the dust to rise and fly very high from the face of the earth; a fierce wind from the sky struggles with the sun, the leaves fall from the lime-tree and land on the ground, and all the grass which was previously green grows faded; then everything that has grown in the beginning ripens and rots, and so the year runs past in many a yesterday, and winter returns, as indeed nature requires.

The sense of autumn's urgency and struggle is very appropriate to Gawain's predicament, for he goes to face a moral test of faithfulness and courage which will apparently lead to his death, and ultimately to the eternal judgement of his conduct; while the seasons repeat their cycle, man has only one chance to achieve his spiritual harvest, for the sequence of the seasons of man's life occurs only once.

Many medieval people viewed autumn in a more positive light. Unless famine struck (and it was often perilously close throughout the middle ages) autumn was a time for full bellies and for feasting before the harshness of winter bit. This more cheerful aspect of the season is depicted in the traditional Labours of the Months. There the autumn months, September, October and November, are given over to illustrations of threshing cereal crops (more usually in manuscripts illustrated in England, where the cereal harvest came a little later than its Continental counterpart), of picking, treading and barrelling up the vintage, and of fattening and killing those animals which were not to be overwintered. Not only had the current year's produce to be preserved and processed, but the following year's produce also had to be ensured. Illustrations of the

Within the farm enclosure two peasants thresh the
grain on the bare earth while a third winnows it to
separate the wheat and the chaff

Labours of the Months therefore depict ploughing and sowing winter
cereal crops.

Autumn's agrarian activities began with the conclusion of the
processing of the grain harvest, a process which had its own mysteries:
winnowing, fanning, casting and threshing, depending on the nature of
the grain and the destination of the end-product, for malting, as seed-
corn, for bread-making or for other culinary purposes. Much of the work
was carried out by peasants bound to do such labour for their lords. As the
weather deteriorated, threshing could be carried out indoors. Men with
jointed wooden flails threshed the grain on the earth floor of huge barns.
Inadequate threshing could mean that foreign bodies were left in the straw;
these could sprout if the straw was used for thatch, or germinate in store.
Winnowing was an outdoor activity, done on windy days; handfuls of corn
were thrown up into the air so the wind could separate the wheat and the
chaff. The heavier grain which fell to the ground could then be shovelled
into storage bins while the chaff could be reserved to feed draught animals.
Some unthreshed grain could be kept and threshed as required, which
eased the immediate workload. Both processes, threshing and winnowing,
were carefully overseen by manorial officials to ensure that the yield was

maintained and to prevent theft. Clearly thieving was common; one Book of Husbandry instructs that care should be taken that the threshers and winnowers do not take corn and carry it away in their dress, boots, shoes and pockets. Nothing was wasted; even the chaff had value, mixed with some corn, as winter fodder for horses.

Commonplace agricultural tasks find their way into literature. In the fifteenth-century English morality play *Mankind*, the vice-figure Mischief rudely interrupts the virtuous teacher Mercy, who has been speaking of the Last Judgement in traditional harvest imagery as an occasion for separating the corn (the virtuous souls) from the chaff (the sinful souls). Mercy asks why Mischief has inflicted his unwanted presence; the vice cheekily replies:

> For a winter corn-thresher, sir, I have hired,
> And ye said the corn should be saved and the chaff should be fired,
> And he proveth nay, as it showeth this verse:
> *Corn servit bredibus, chaff horsibus, straw firibusque.*
> [Nonsense-Latin: 'Corn serves for bread, chaff for horses, straw for fires']
> This is as much to say, to your lewd understanding,
> As the corn shall serve to bread at the next baking;
> *Chaff horsibus et reliqua.*
> [Nonsense-Latin: 'Chaff for the horses etcetera']
> The chaff to horse shall be a good provent [fodder]
> When a man is for-cold the straw may be burnt,
> And so forth, etcetera.

The more prosaic agricultural rhymer, Thomas Tusser, put it more succinctly: 'No chaff in the bin makes the horse look thin.'

Opposite: One thresher uses a jointed wooden flail to beat the stalks while the other winnows. This process was less wasteful in a proper covered threshing barn. Below: Winnowing was hard work, as is shown by the efforts of this peasant

Mills, vital to the community for processing its grain, were a crucial part of the country landscape and of the agrarian economy, but few things can have caused more problems in many villages. The investment in the construction of a mill was substantial. Tenants were bound to support the lord's mill by taking their grain there to be ground and turned into flour, an activity for which they had to pay one sixteenth of their precious harvest. While many households may have had a little handmill to grind flour for domestic consumption, possession of handmills was often forbidden.

The workings of this powerful water-wheel can be clearly seen.
It had a substantial capacity for grinding grain but would be
badly affected by drought

In most places, villagers were obliged to use the lord's mill for
grinding their corn. Carrying the grain to the mill was hard
physical work, frequently undertaken by women

Millers were proverbially dishonest: 'An honest miller hath a golden
thumb'! Chaucer's Miller, an incongruous pilgrim to Canterbury, knows
all about corn-stealing and overcharging on toll-payments. Such thieving
is portrayed in Chaucer's grotesquely farcical 'Reeve's Tale', in which the
dishonest miller of Trumpington cheats two Cambridge students bringing
their college's grain to him, and is in turn punished with a beating-up and
with the defilement of his wife and daughter.

Mills were used for all sorts of purposes, most widely for grinding grain
for baking and brewing, but additionally for pressing olives or nuts to
extract oil, and for cloth-processing. In the early middle ages mills were
powered by water diverted from a fast-flowing stream into a mill-pond
whose sides were banked up with clay, a system of floodgates and sluices
helping to regulate the flow of water. Water power was valuable, but
problems could arise. The flow of water might not be consistently swift;
Tusser advised his readers to take their grist (corn for grinding) to the mill

Women often played a key role in the grape harvest. Here, ripe
purple grapes are transferred from the pickers' baskets into a
wicker 'back-pack' to be carried to the wine-press

and ensure they kept ground grain in stock 'lest the miller lack water as
many do'. In winter mill ponds frequently froze, immobilizing the mill. In
many parts of Europe there was either insufficient water or, as in the
fenlands of England, insufficient gradient to ensure an adequate supply of
power, problems to which the windmill provided the ideal solution. It was
necessary to ensure that the vanes of the windmill faced the correct way to
take advantage of the wind direction: this was achieved by mounting the
whole windmill on a swivelling post, which accounts for the odd
appearance, to modern eyes, of many windmills shown in medieval rural
scenes. Mills were as common in the landscape as churches, so the
frequency with which they are illustrated is not surprising.

The grape harvest and the processes of wine production were popular
autumn subjects in Labours of the Months illustrations, both in England
and on the Continent, though towards the end of the medieval period
wine production was in decline in England. Earlier, vineyards had

The grapes arrive at the wine-press and the juice is
expressed by treading in huge vats

flourished in England even as far north as Yorkshire, and notably in the
vale of Gloucester. However, English grapes grew on the edge of the area
of Europe in which vines could then survive and bear fruit, and so they
were very vulnerable to small climatic changes. In the fourteenth century
a small but appreciable change in Britain's climate led to cooler, damper
summers, which made successful commercial vine-growing much harder.
Vines continued to exist in private gardens and estates during the fifteenth
century, but had become unusual by the latter half of the sixteenth.
Fortunately the wine trade with the Continent, especially the Rhineland
and France, was by then well established, and prices were within the reach
of the comfortably-off. In 1342 the price of Gascon wine in England was
fourpence per gallon and Rhenish sixpence per gallon. Those who could
afford them preferred the sweeter or more robust Continental wines in any
case, for English wines were regarded as sharp and inferior even when
sweetened with honey and spices (at least according to foreigners; though
the twelfth-century historian William of Malmesbury maintained that
Gloucestershire wine was very good).

Poorer folk would rarely taste wine in their lifetime; at feasts held by the
manorial lord, they were grateful for good-quality ale. Cider was easily
produced in areas where apples were plentiful, and perry could be made
from fermented pear-juice. In most of Europe, however, the major native
alcoholic drink was unhopped ale, of which most people drank on average
five or six pints a day. Little water was drunk. Ale came in a wide range of
qualities from the poorest people's drink to the grandest, such as that taken

A manorial lord overseeing many of the processes of viticulture.
On the left a new row of vines is being planted whilst in the
middle ground the grapes are being picked from established vines

as a present by Thomas Becket to France on an ambassadorial journey in 1158. Ale was made from malted grain and was commonly brewed even in small households. Wheat, oats or barley were ordinarily used, although the French are known to have brewed from unlikely-sounding ingredients including vetches, lentils and rye. Ale was not subject to seasonal production like wine, except in so far as very special ales were brewed in households and institutions to mature well in advance of particular festivals. In large households with ample storage facilities, brewing tended to be concentrated in spring (March) and autumn (October), but in smaller concerns more frequent brewings took place.

Beer, made with hops, came from Flanders to England in the later fourteenth century, with Flemish brewers settling in London in the fifteenth century, but it did not catch on quickly beyond London.

The moment of reckoning has come for this hapless ox which
should provide a considerable amount of meat from its carcase.
In the doorway, the woman who will have to process the
resultant meat products waits in anticipation

For animals as well as humans, autumn was a time of plenty, as they were fattened for slaughter. Autumn was the time for culling animals, and many cattle, sheep and goats were killed then, because winter fodder was in short supply and expensive. Valuable reserves of food had to be kept for the crucial draught animals and in times of shortage these could not be used for animals merely intended to provide fresh meat for the table. The slaughtered beasts provided both fresh meat and salted meats for the winter; stock for breeding and dairy purposes, working beasts like draught oxen and those animals intended to provide a kind of 'walking larder' ready for slaughter later in the winter were kept back from the autumn cull.

Once the harvest was over, the animals were allowed to wander over the communal fields, eating what they could of the stubble. Cattle were allowed to graze before sheep, for the latter cropped so close that there was little left after them. Poultry would also be fattened at this time. 'Stubble geese', killed before they had begun to lose the fat gathered from eating the grains dropped by careless harvesters, had a considerable reputation as a gastronomic delight.

November was known to the Anglo-Saxons as the 'blood month'. Labours of the Months illustrations often show hogs being fattened in October or November and killed in the following month. Pigs were common in every village: lean, coarse-haired animals who lived for most of the year on scraps and what they could forage. No animal so easily put on flesh; it was reckoned that a pig that needed to be fed on grain was not worth keeping. In a mild winter the animals could forage out of doors at

Many typical autumn activities are going on at once in this fine
painting from the Golf Book of Hours

least until Christmas and be slaughtered as needed, thus providing fresh
pork, more palatable than the tougher salted and smoked meat. Similarly,
some sheep were held back from the cull; they could always be butchered
later if fodder ran short. The mild English climate was well suited to sheep-
keeping; unless the winter was very harsh, sheep could remain out of
doors, protected and contained by folds made of wooden hurdles. These
folds would be moved regularly, ensuring that the lord's land was
systematically dunged with sheep-droppings.

Killing the pig, singeing the carcase and cutting hams from the
flesh – all part of the process of ensuring the winter food supply

Dealing with the meat and animal products of the autumn slaughter involved a great deal of work. The usual methods of preserving meat were salting, smoking and hanging, which preserved the muscular meats well. Beef, mutton and pork from animals slaughtered in November could be prepared for keeping over the winter by steeping the flesh in brine for several days and then hanging it up in a dry or smoky atmosphere, perhaps the chimney or the smoke-hole. When the time came to eat it, hard salt-beef or mutton was not very palatable and had to be simmered in water for a long time to get rid of some of the salt. Salt bacon would be boiled and added to pottage with plenty of herbs to make it into a passable meal. Pork, which absorbed less salt, remained more succulent, perhaps another reason for the universal popularity of the pig among the peasantry. Pigs provided the family with a variety of meat products for preservation and consumption over the winter. Bacon was rubbed with spices, salt or honey before smoking. Offal presented a more immediate disposal problem, as did blood and bone-marrow; they provided treats for peasant families at the time of the killing. Various types of sausage and blood-puddings were the seasonal delicacies of pig-killing time, providing ways of using up the fat, soft organs and blood, well-spiced, blended with onion or garlic, and stuffed into lengths of intestine or the larger guts of the animal. Pigs also provided vital lard and the tallow necessary for the making of candles.

Nature also offered her own uncultivated harvest. The hedgerows provided rich sources of nutrition: hips, haws, wild berries, wild apples, plums and nuts cost nothing beyond the time it took to collect them. The

Even the hunt yielded valuable food which could be stored in preparation for the long winter months. Here, the lord brings home a carcase slung across his horse while in the background, manorial servants attend to a variety of autumnal tasks

After preparing the ground, the sower is following
the ploughed furrows as he carefully dispenses the right
quantity of seed to ensure the correct density of crop
and prevent weeds from growing

natural harvest also yielded produce for uses other than eating: reeds and osiers were collected, to be plaited into baskets and rough nets later in the winter; rushes were picked for use as candle-wicks; and nettles were gathered for making into thread (they could also be used instead of flax in the manufacture of a very durable linen-like cloth).

As if laying up and processing food supplies for the winter did not keep people busy enough in autumn, there were many necessary tasks to be done to ensure that the next year would be productive. Awareness of the importance of autumn's preparatory labours was not limited to farmers or agricultural theorists, for everyone was ultimately dependent on the outcome. Thomas Usk, author of *The Treatise of Love*, speaks of the 'time when October begins to take its leave and November comes into view' as the time when 'good land-tillers work the earth with great travail, to bring forth more corn for man's sustenance, for the following year'. Thomas Tusser's agricultural instructions for September tell the farmer firmly: 'Thresh seed and to fanning, September doth cry. /Get plough to the field, and be sowing of rye.' Care was necessary in sowing, as Tusser warns: 'See corn sown in /Too thick nor too thin. /For want of seed /Land yieldeth weed.' He recommends October for the sowing of white wheat, but not in rain, and preferably in the right kind of soil ('All gravel and sand /Is not the best land. /A rottenly mould /Is land worth gold.'). Garlic and beans can be sown in November (Tusser recommends St Edmund's Day, 20 November); saints' days often served as useful reminders to perform tasks in the agricultural calendar.

Every village had its swineherd whose duty in autumn it was to collect the villagers' pigs and drive them up to the pasture or into the woodland to search for food – nuts, berries, hips and haws. Pigs were particularly fond of acorns and beech mast. Books of Husbandry suggest that a well-looked-after sow would farrow five times in two years and would produce up to seven piglets each time. Sows after farrowing and runt piglets could be kept on refuse while hard frost and bad weather lasted. Walter of Henley suggested that only in February, March and April did pigs need to be given supplementary food. However, pigs did need to be carefully watched, for they could burrow under fences and do considerable damage. It was important for the swineherd to keep them out of fields in harvest time; men were regularly fined by village courts for allowing their beasts to do

Hive maintenance required good protective clothing as worn by
these late-medieval Italian beekeepers. Wicker and wooden
hives can be seen here, raised above ground level for protection
against vermin and weather

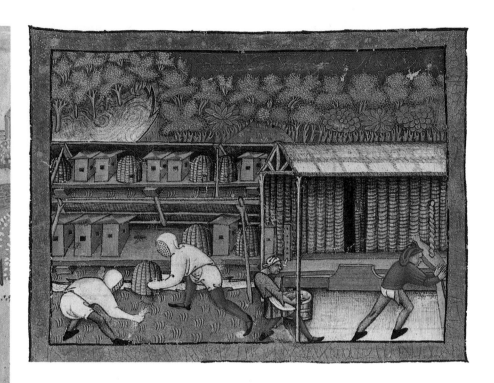

damage. Village by-laws emphasized that no one should have pigs or
piglets outside his house except in good custody. In summer and early
autumn, hog-ringers were employed to put rings through the animals'
noses to prevent their destructive burrowing and rooting.

Sheep too required vigilant attention in autumn. They were prone to
illnesses, primarily the scab and the liver-fluke. The former could be cured
by the application of a little tar, hence the origin of the saying, 'don't spoil
the sheep for a half-pence worth of tar', nowadays popularly
misunderstood as referring to ships rather than sheep! Tar was among the
crucial items to be purchased for which a peasant required ready cash,

Opposite below: Coarse-haired, ridge-backed hogs are making
the most of a windfall from the orchard. In the autumn, pigs,
like other animals, were being fattened for slaughter

perhaps obtained from selling wool. Fluke was caught from a mildew, and the autumn was a dangerous period as sheep might eat the mildew on leaves, or the snails which harboured it.

Even the bee-hives needed attention to ensure that the bees were getting adequate nourishment. Tusser suggested that the weight of the hive be checked and the bees fed if necessary: 'Go look to thy bees; if the hive be too light, /set water and honey with rosemary dight [prepared]./ Which set in a dish full of sticks in the hive, /from danger of famine, yea save them alive.' Famine among the bees was a particular danger with new hives where the young bees had had less time to store up food than a well-established hive. It was estimated that eight swarms could be supported for a whole winter with one gallon of honey.

The autumn months were the time for various arduous but necessary preparatory, conservational and tidying activities, such as trenching and ditching, repairing walls, removing molehills, cleaning out the farmyard (and the privies, which Tusser recommends should be done at midnight to cause the least offence!), and muckspreading of both animal and human waste (the latter particularly recommended for trenching in the garden). Such unpleasant work cannot have been very popular, especially since its rewards became apparent only in the long term rather than immediately. One anonymous motet expresses a firm preference for a lazy and luxurious life in the city rather than the hard grind of agriculture:

> Some talk of threshing and winnowing, digging and ploughing but I care nothing for these sports; for there is no life so good as to be well supplied with good clear wine and capons and to be with good companions, happy and joyous, singing, joking and making love and to have whatever you need for your pleasure and fair ladies to your liking. And all this can be found in Paris.

Before the evenings began to shorten dramatically, there was also time in autumn for informal celebrations and social events. Many villages had 'ales', a type of social event often organized by the lord, which all had to attend and indeed to contribute small sums of money. The tenants of Glastonbury were obliged to appear at the 'ale' and drink at their own expense. 'Ales' were excuses for heavy drinking and for dancing and

The owner and his steward check to ensure that they are
producing good, clear wine. A screw-operated wine-press is
being worked in the middle ground

These youths are playing a version of hockey with a large ball,
probably made from a pig's bladder

games, and the licentiousness which could result attracted the disapproval of the church. Condemnations of dancing by medieval preachers included fulminations against lewd kissing and illicit sexual activity; many preachers also condemned the village ale-house, describing it as the 'devil's chapel'.

The practical activities of the seasons, as well as the weather, had their influence on children's games. As the late medieval poet Alexander Barclay put it when discussing boy's games, 'Each time and season has its delight and joys.' Barclay described football as an autumn pastime for children because of the availability of the bladders of slaughtered pigs as handballs (all the more fun with dried beans or peas rattling inside them) and footballs. Some children's games depended on the absence of daylight; one late medieval English poet draws a poignant analogy for humans' limited perceptions of the ultimate realities of life from the game children play when at night they chase shadows cast by a candle along a wall. Froissart tells of how, when the moon was bright, he would play a game called 'Pinch me'. In summer and autumn, playfulness found very many opportunities to tip over into mischief and petty theft, as we saw in the fifteenth-century English poet Lydgate's description of childhood scrumping in the chapter on summer.

Ecclesiastical celebrations could be complemented by secular junketings on several major festivals, not just at Christmas; the feast of All Saints, though not as great as that of Pentecost, is a notable example. Literary presentations of the aristocratic world of Arthurian romance often

The sombre ceremony of a Requiem Mass is being celebrated
with due decorum. The covered catafalque is flanked by
candles and praying figures

use such occasions of elaborate feasting as structurally important points in
the adventures of Arthurian knights; for example, in *Sir Gawain and the
Green Knight* King Arthur gives a great feast on All Saints' (or All
Hallows') Day, 1 November, also marking the imminent departure of
Gawain on the following day, the sombre feast of All Souls, to keep his
probably fatal promise to receive a return blow from the magical Green

Knight. Gawain's send-off matches in 'splendid revelry of the Round Table' the earlier New Year feast which was described with much pomp and ceremony:

> Then the first course came in with blasts from trumpets with many very brightly-coloured banners hanging from them; there rose up the sound of drums and splendid pipes and loud, exuberant skirlings wakened the echoes, so that many a heart was greatly roused by their music. In addition very elaborate dishes were served with an abundance of fresh meat, and on so many platters that it was difficult to find room in front of the guests to put down on the tablecloth the silver dishes holding the various stews . . . Each pair of guests shared twelve dishes, with excellent beer and bright wine too.

Forms of secular entertainment other than feasting could celebrate a major church festival; for example, an important All Hallowmas tournament, attended by numerous tributary kings, occurs near the end of Sir Thomas Malory's fifteenth-century prose romance *Le Morte D'Arthur*.

Hallowmas, a sanctification of a great pre-Christian autumnal feast, had been adopted by the church to become the feast of All Saints and All Souls, 1–2 November, a great feast in honour of the dead. All Saints' Day was in honour of all the saints, known and unknown. It was a holy day, a holiday and an occasion for special masses and liturgical ceremonies. In this way, saints whose particular day was not otherwise marked might be honoured. Prayers to the saints would ease an individual's path both through life and in the transition to the next world. It was appropriate therefore that the feast of All Saints was immediately followed by that of All Souls, commemorating all the faithful departed. Prayers on this day were particularly efficacious in helping souls which had not yet progressed from purgatory to heaven, and the existence of All Souls' Day provided reassurance for people too poor to pay for thousands of masses to be said posthumously to assist the passage of their souls through purgatory to heaven. Graves of friends and relatives were visited. In many towns men arrayed in black would roam the streets, ringing handbells and exhorting people to remember souls in purgatory and aid them with prayers. Such customs were a powerful reminder of the more sombre message of autumn.

WINTER

Winter was the season when the work of the whole year could be assessed by the comfort, or lack of it, which forethought, hard labour and good or bad luck brought:

> Winter all eats
> That summer begets
> [Winter consumes all that summer produces]

as a Middle English aphorism goes. In the *Secretum Secretorum*, it began in mid-December when the sun entered the sign of Capricorn, and lasted until mid-March, when the sun entered Aries. During the period of the year when nights are longest and days shortest, 'Cold is predominant, the winds are piercing, all the leaves fall from the trees, and all green things die and grow hard as stones,' it says, and animals, too, feel the pinch: 'Most beasts keep to mountain caves, because of the very great cold and damp of the season; the air is dark, the period is gloomy, and the animals shiver, because the season weakens their bodily strength.' The *Secretum* goes on to compare winter to an old woman, afflicted and decrepit with age, lacking clothes and nearing death.

The dominant 'humour' of winter is phlegm, cold and moist; to counteract its deleterious effects, the *Secretum* once again recommends a modification of diet. It prescribes hot foods, such as pigeons, mutton and other roasts, fatty foods, figs, nuts, fine red wines and hot potions, to combat phlegm. Laxatives and bloodletting are to be avoided where possible, as are overeating and overindulgence in lovemaking. Hot liniments for rubbing the body, on the other hand, will do good. One version of the *Secretum*, perhaps conscious that it is somewhat puritanical, qualifies its prescriptions by saying that, actually, overindulgence in winter is not quite so detrimental as in other seasons, since the body's natural heat is drawn inwards in that season, resulting in good digestion. It is as good a way as any to justify Christmas cheer!

Whatever relief winter might receive in the form of Christmas festivities, its practical discomforts and the general emotionally depressing effect of the season are vigorously expressed by medieval writers. A terse early Middle English lyric, for which we still have the melody, complains of the discomfort of winter's coming in comparison with the pleasure of spring, implicitly suggesting that the speaker's state of mind is reflected in the season; he is most probably a complaining lover, though the poem could be interpreted as a lament by any human being all too conscious of mortality: 'It is pleasant while spring lasts with bird-song; but now the wind's blast and rough weather are approaching. Ah! alas! how long this night is! And I am most unjustly sorrowing, mourning and fasting.'

Winter's miseries had been endowed with symbolic religious significance from an early date, as in the theologian Hrabanus Maurus's comment that 'winter indeed signifies tribulation, or the end of mortal life.' Christian teaching may have reinforced the moral interpretation of the season, but the natural and long-established perception of human mortality reflected in the dead season of the year had ancient roots. Penitential teaching seized on this emotionally compelling correspondence to strengthen its lessons, producing some moving meditations like this Middle English lyric:

Winter awakens all my sorrow, now that the leafy branches are growing bare; often I sigh and sorrowfully mourn when I consider how all this world's joy comes to nothing. One moment it is here, and the next, gone as if it had indeed never existed. What many people say is true: Everything is transient except the will of God. We all have to die, however little that may please us. All that grows green in the grove is now withering all at once. Jesus, help to make that [lesson] clear, and protect us from hell, for I do not know where I must go, or how long I must remain here.

Winter was undoubtedly an intrinsically unpleasant season for medieval people; the best they could hope for was to mitigate its discomfort by forethought about food, heating and shelter. When some major natural disaster or human disruption, such as warfare, intervened, the consequences could be appalling misery. Even without cataclysms and

Energetic pruning of vines with a variety of implements

disasters, winter was a grim experience for the poor. The fourteenth-century poet William Langland speaks compassionately in *Piers Plowman* of the miserable lot of the needy, 'the poor in the cottage, burdened with a crew of children and with a landlord's rent' who, along with their hungry, crying babies ' . . . themselves suffer painfully with hunger in winter, getting up at night to rock the cradle in a cramped room'.

The difficulties of winter were still felt, even if in less fundamental ways, by the well-to-do; in a late fifteenth-century letter from Edward Plumpton to his cousin Sir Robert Plumpton, he apologizes for sending no wildfowl as a luxury gift: ' . . . for in all Lancashire none could be had for any money.

A child sucks at its mother's breast in the warmth indoors,
while outside firewood is being chopped. These peasants share
their cottage with their livestock although they are clearly
relatively prosperous

A boar-hunt in progress in a snowy landscape. Boars were the
principal quarry hunted by the upper classes in winter

The snow and frost were so great that there was none in the country, but
they had flown away to sea; and that prevented me from sending any as I
had promised.' Even life at court was unpleasant in winter. Eustache
Deschamps (1348–1407), a poet employed by the French king, described
its miseries:

Four months every year . . . have been too cold for me ever since my
childhood: November is one of them, then December and January,
and after that February, the great promoter of colds. In this cold
weather it is best to keep away [from court]. For then come frosts and
snows and rains and winds in great confusion; then the king goes off
to hunt the boar, and the officers in attendance blow on their hands;
each one keeps his belly well wrapped up, and they swing their arms
to drive out the cold. . . . Young page-boys out in the woods weep for
cold and cannot hold the horses' bridles. As for the courtiers'
lodgings, God knows how cold they are and how grudgingly the fuel is
doled out; in hall everyone shivers, servants and squires are not
permitted to wear cloaks.

Fodder saved for winter feeding is being distrbuted to the farm
animals. Pigeons and doves wait hopefully on the roofs
of surrounding buildings. Lower: Flax, harvested in summer, is
being processed and prepared by women before being spun into
linen thread, an activity for winter days

Over much of Europe, little agrarian activity could take place in winter,
and illuminations of Labours of the Months for the months of December,
January and February show mostly indoor scenes. The winter wheat was
sown by All Hallows; henceforth the ground would be either frozen or too
muddy to work. None the less, there were a number of important
preparatory works to be done in the countryside, designed either to
preserve the health of animals over the winter period or to ensure that the
community was ready for the onset of spring and the rebirth of the agrarian
year. Winter tasks carried out by peasants on their lord's land included
sawing timber, cutting twigs for hurdles and to repair the ewe-house, and
gathering bracken for the byres. If the clay banks of the mill-pond had
been eroded in a wet autumn, they would have to be repaired. A major

Equipped with curved knives, this man cuts and collects
branches which could be used for fencing or burning.
His wife is making neat bundles of the wood

activity of the season was watching over those animals which had to
survive the winter in a healthy state, to be ready to work in the spring.
Corn stubble saved from the harvest was mixed with straw to enrich the
fodder fed to draught animals. In bad weather sheep had to be brought into
the ewe-houses and fed on coarse straw; if there was a shortage of hay, the
pods and straw of peas could be used. The shepherd's year began early, for
young lambs were born as early as January and had to be protected from
vermin and foxes as well as from the elements. Some were sold young;
those which were to be retained as part of the flock were left with their
mothers until May.

If outdoor activities over the winter months were mostly those of repair
and reconstruction, the same was true of indoor activities. Many peasant
families took advantage of the time to be spent indoors to prepare for the
spring. Wooden spoons, platters and bowls were carved. Horn and leather
mugs were repaired. Reeds and rushes were plaited into baskets, harnesses
and rudimentary fish creels; farm tools were repaired; harrow teeth were
cut from ash or willow and sharpened. Women were equally busy, spinning
and sewing, and repairing and replacing household equipment and
garments.

Women were also faced with the pressing problem of feeding their
families, perhaps trying to provide some variety from the monotony of the
winter diet which set in as autumn food stocks began to decline. The staple
food for peasant families was pottage, cooked in a metal pot hung over the
fire, in which very common additional ingredients were onions, peas,
beans, leeks, colewort and lentils. A wide variety of herbs gathered in the

In this comfortable interior, it appears that the winter problems
of feeding the household have been overcome. The woman
carries in a roast bird. Even the cat looks contented

wilds or grown in the cottage garden might be used for flavour; parsley was
particularly important. The pottage might be enriched with stock from
boiled meat, fish or poultry, and on occasion some smoked or salted meat
was added as a treat. The winter diet was highly salted, for as well as
occasional meat, the staples of the peasant winter diet, cheese and butter,
had also been salted to preserve them through the winter. Many peasant
families had a few hens whose eggs, roasted in their shells or fried, provided
some variety on non-fast days.

A well-bred young woman disregards distractions and
perseveres with spinning her thread. Lower: A farmhand
spreads with his pitchfork the fodder which he has carted to the
fields to feed the livestock

'Disport', pastimes and amusements, helped to keep winter depression
at bay and, equally practically, helped people to keep warm. The late
medieval poet Alexander Barclay speaks in his Winter *Eclogue* of football
and other active ball-games played, as in the previous season, by both boys
and men. According to Barclay:

Each one contendeth and hath a great delight
With foot and with hand the bladder for to smite:
If it fall to ground they lift it up again,
This wise to labour they count it for no pain,
Running and leaping they drive away the cold,
The sturdy ploughmen lusty, strong, and bold,
Overcometh the winter with driving the foot ball,
Forgetting labour and many a grievous fall.

129

Other active outdoor games included throwing of stones and of bars of wood and iron. Quoits was chiefly popular among the labouring classes: an iron pin was driven into the ground at which teams threw their quoits. Also popular was a form of rounders called 'Prisoners' Bars'; King Edward III prohibited it from being played in the avenues of the palace of Westminster during sessions of parliament. During the Hundred Years' War, parliament forbade the playing of a number of popular games, including handball, quoits and kayles, stating that men and boys should practise archery instead. Children's games included marbles, using small stones or nuts; rough-and-tumble wrestling on pick-a-back; whipping tops; bobbing for apples on a string; and blind-man's-buff. A fall of snow must have given pleasure to children then as now. When ponds or rivers froze over, both children and adults enjoyed skating, using crude skates made of animal bones or polished wood.

A number of indoor games existed which passed the time on long winter evenings. Games of chance and gambling were popular. The surviving account books of Henry VII's Queen, Elizabeth of York, are full of repayments to her ladies for gambling debts. In all secular households ladies and gentlemen indulged in it; chamber servants were often called upon to pay gambling debts out of their own pockets. Backgammon, with its mixture of skill and chance, was one of the most popular board games. Attempts were made to prevent the lower classes from dicing and gambling, but the very frequency of prohibitions testifies to their lack of success. Chess, which became popular from the twelfth century, was widely played; it was taken very seriously and often led to violent altercations.

> One day a dispute arose over a knight which had been taken. One said it was a fair move while the other claimed that it was false. As often happens in this game where even the wisest get impatient, hot words followed. Indeed both sprang to their feet in anger reaching for their poignards [daggers] and spoiling for a fight . . . and all on account of a trifling piece of ivory carved in the likeness of a knight.

An idealized picture of a comfortable winter evening comes from an anonymous French motet: 'By the fireside, in the cold month of January, I

Three children enjoy the timeless joys of snowballing.
In the background, a pack-animal is carrying grain to be
ground by the windmill. The wooden mill is mounted
on a swivelling post so that it can be turned to take
advantage of changes in the wind-direction

like to eat salt meat and fat capons; a well dressed lady, and singing and
merrymaking, that is what pleases me, with good wine in plenty, a bright
fire that does not smoke, dice and a board, and no quarrelling.'

The tedium of winter was broken by the great festival of Christmas. For
those who laboured on the land it was the longest period of respite from
work in the fields, a high spot in the dark gloom of winter. It was the
culmination of the season of plenty; after Christmas the weather would
worsen and belt-tightening would begin in earnest, the diet becoming
more monotonous as food stocks diminished. Much of the emphasis at
Christmas time was on rich and poor celebrating together, the rich
opening their doors to the less fortunate in honour of Christ's birth. There
were practical reasons for this: Thomas Tusser explains that the poor
suffered more in winter because there was little demand for casual labour:
'what season then better, of all the whole year, /thy needy poor neighbour

A vigorous game of handball in the foreground does not appear
to disturb the chess-players seated in the covered walk

to comfort and cheer?' Usually a feast was provided for the peasantry by the
lord but peasants were also expected to contribute something, perhaps a
chicken or loaves. There is a description of a Christmas dinner held for the
peasants on a Glastonbury abbey manor, when each peasant was entitled
to the following:

> He ought to have his dinner at Christmas in the Lord's court; himself
> and his wife, that is two white loaves of bread and two dishes of meat
> and sufficient ale, clearly and honourably. And he ought to bring
> with him a dish and a cup and a table cloth. And he ought to bring
> before Christmas one bundle of firewood to cook his dish. And if he
> does not do this he shall have his victual uncooked.

The stipulation that the peasant bring some fuel for the cooking of his meal
was commonly found elsewhere.

132

Feasting at Christmas time

A Christmas celebration in a noble household. Men and
women dressed in the height of fashion dance to music provided
by a small wind band

Among the Christmas fare recommended by Tusser was good drink, a
good fire in the hall, brawn, pudding, sauce, mustard, beef, mutton and
pork, mince pies, pig, goose, veal, capon and turkey, cheese, apples and
nuts, accompanied by carols. Clearly the twelve days of Christmas were a
time of merriment, the atmosphere summed up by the words of a fifteenth-
century carol:

Make we merry both rich and poor,
For now is the time of Christmas!

Let no man come into this hall,
Groom, page, nor yet marshal,
But that some sport he bring withal!
For now is the time of Christmas!

If that he say he cannot sing,
Some other sport then let him bring!
That it may please at this feasting
For now is the time of Christmas!

If he say, he can nought do,
Then for my love ask him no mo!
But to the stocks then let him go!
For now is the time of Christmas!

Comfortably-off townsfolk gather in preparation for some
Christmas festivities

A member of a prominent Norfolk family, Margery Paston, writing in 1484, explained to her husband what games and Christmas activities were considered acceptable in the house of a person recently bereaved. While noisy activities were not permissible, chess and cards were allowed:

> I sent your eldest son to my Lady Morley to find out what sports took place in her house during the Christmas after the death of . . . her husband; and she said that there were no masked games, or harping, or lute-playing, or singing, or any noisy amusements, but only backgammon, chess and cards. She gave her people permission to play such games, and nothing else.

In the royal household and in other noble households a lord of misrule or lord of fools would be chosen. John Stow claimed that

> a lord of misrule, or master of merry disports, and the like had ye in the house of every nobleman of honour or good worship . . . These lords beginning their rule on All Hallows Eve, continued the same till the morrow after the feast of the Purification, commonly called Candlemas Day. In all which space there were fine and subtle disguising, masks, and mummeries, with playing at cards for counters, nails, and points, in every house, more for pastime than for gain.

Christmas trees are a Victorian importation from Germany, but throughout the middle ages men and women decorated their houses in green whenever possible. Stow says: 'Against the feast of Christmas every man's house, as also the parish churches, were decked with holm [holly], ivy, bays, and whatsoever the season of the year afforded to be green.' The greenery functioned as a reminder of spring and of the rebirth of the year, and in religious terms symbolized eternal life. A further reminder of the year's resurgence was to be found on the day after Epiphany (6 January, the feast of the Three Kings) when, although it was too early to begin ploughing again, many places had traditional agricultural ceremonies to mark the resumption of the farming year. Frequently the plough and the distaff, traditional symbols of male and female activities respectively, were honoured. Plough races or a village procession with a plough might take place. The church authorities were clearly unhappy about the strong hold which ceremonies with pagan origins had on rural communities. In *Dives and Pauper*, a fifteenth-century treatise on the Ten Commandments, the church condemns those who mark the beginning of the year by drawing their ploughs around bonfires to bring good luck. Little more could happen in the fields until Candlemas marked the real resumption of tillage.

At Candlemas, the Feast of the Purification of the Virgin Mary took the place of one of the ancient heathen quarterly feasts. All over Europe, men and women walked in processions in honour of the Purification of the Virgin Mary. This ceremony marked the end of the winter's respite from labour in the fields. Once Candlemas was over, tilling the earth could start again. The agrarian year had turned full circle and spring was at hand.

This party appears to be a little out-of-hand. It is a medieval
representation of ancient Rome dining customs but it gives a
good idea of some of the cruder aspects of medieval festivities

ACKNOWLEDGEMENTS

The sources of quotations in the text derived from published works are as follows:

p.13 quoted in G.G Coulton, *Social Life in Britain from the Conquest to the Reformation*, (Cambridge, 1918) pp.52–3.

p.31 quoted in John Harthan, *Books of Hours and their owners* (London, 1977) p.35.

p.40 translated in Helen Waddell, *Medieval Latin lyrics* (Oxford, 1929) p.223.

p.42 translated in Helen Waddell, *Medieval Latin lyrics*, p.169.

pp.52-3 quoted in W. E. Mead, *The English medieval feast* (London, 1931) p.221.

p.55 quoted in J. J. Jusserand, *English wayfaring life* (1889: reprinted Bath, 1970) p.43.

p.64 Hrabanus Maurus, quoted in Rosemond Tuve, *Seasons and months: studies in a tradition of Middle English poetry* (1933: reissued Cambridge and Totowa, New Jersey, 1974) p.129.

p.75 quoted in W. Endrei and L. Zolnay, trs. Károly Ravasz, rev. Bertha Gaster, *Fun and games in old Europe* (Budapest, 1986) p.85.

p.75 quoted in Edith Rickert, *Chaucer's world* (New York, 1948) pp. 226–7 (Stow Quotation).

p.81 *The Penguin book of French verse to the fifteenth century* ed. Brian Woledge (Harmondsworth, 1966) pp.216–17.

p.85 *The master of game. By Edward, second Duke of York* eds. W. A. and F. Baillie-Grohman (London, 1904) p.173.

p.86 Froissart, *Chronicles*, trs. and ed. by G. Brereton (Harmondsworth, 1968) p.386.

p.89 *The Book of Margery Kempe*, modernized by W. Butler-Bowdon, (Oxford, 1936: reprinted in World's Classics, 1954) p.227.

p.92 The monk of Winchcomb, quoted in G. C. Homans, *English villagers of the thirteenth century* (Cambridge, Mass., 1942) p.369.

p.96 Hrabanus Maurus, quoted in Rosemond Tuve, *Seasons and months*, p.129.

p.115 *The Penguin book of French verse to the fifteenth century*, p.207.

p.117 The children's shadow-game is referred to in 'Think on Yesterday' in Carleton Brown, ed., *Religious lyrics of the fourteenth century* (Oxford, 1924: corrected 1957) p.143.

pp.123-4 Plumpton letter: from Douglas Gray, ed., *The Oxford book of late medieval verse and prose* (Oxford, 1985) p.45.

p.125 *The Penguin book of French verse to the fifteenth century*, pp.244–45.

p.130 quoted in G. Hindley, *The medieval establishment 1200–1500* (London, 1970) p.57.

pp.130-1 *The Penguin book of French verse to the fifteenth century*, p.206.

p.132 quoted in H. S. Bennett, *Life on the English manor: a study of peasant conditions* (Cambridge, 1937) p.263.

Other quotations which appear in the text have been modernized or translated from editions of Middle English works as follows:

Larry D. Benson, ed., *The Riverside Chaucer* (Oxford, 1988).

R. T. Davies, ed., *Medieval English lyrics: a critical anthology* (London, 1963).

Mark Eccles, ed., *The Macro plays*, Early English Text Society 262 (London, 1969) (for *Mankind*).

James Gairdner, ed., *The Paston letters* (Gloucester, 1983).

E. V. Gordon, ed., *The Pearl* (Oxford, 1953).

Douglas Gray, ed., *The Oxford book of late medieval verse and prose* (Oxford, 1985).

M. C. Seymour, ed., *Selections from Hoccleve* (Oxford, 1981).

G. V. Smithers, ed., *Kyng Alisaunder*, Early English Text Society 227 and 237 (Oxford, 1952–7).

H. N. MacCracken, ed., *The minor poems of John Lydgate*, Early English Text Society Original Series 192 and Extra Series 107 (London, 1908–10).

M. A. Manzalaoui, ed., *Secretum Secretorum: nine English versions*, vol. I.: Text, Early English Text Society 276 (Oxford, 1977) esp. the Ashmole version, pp. 56–9.

M. Y. Offord, ed., *The Parlement of the Three Ages*, Early English Text Society 246 (Oxford, 1959).

A. V. C. Schmidt, ed., *The vision of Piers Plowman* (London, 1978).

Celia and Kenneth Sisam, eds, *The Oxford book of medieval English verse* (Oxford, 1970).

W. W. Skeat, ed., *The complete works of Chaucer*, vol. 7 (Oxford, 1897) for Thomas Usk, *The testament of love*.

John Stow, *The survey of London 1603* (London, 1916), with an introduction by H. B. Wheatley.

J. R. R. Tolkien and E. V. Gordon, eds, rev. Norman Davis, *Sir Gawain and the Green Knight* (Oxford, 1967).

Thomas Tusser, *Five hundred points of good husbandry* (Oxford, 1984), with an introduction by Geoffrey Grigson.

Beatrice White, ed., *Barclay's Eclogues*, Early English Text Society 175 (1927: repr. London, 1961).

PICTURE ACKNOWLEDGEMENTS

The illustrations on the cover are from the British Library, London.
Egerton MS 1147 f 9 and f 6v. Book of Hours, Ghent, late 15th cent.
The frontispiece is from the Louvain Town Hall Museum, Belgium. Photo Paul Laes.
1. British Library, London. Royal MS 14 E VI f 204. *Rustican* made for Edward VI, Bruges, 1473-1483.
5. Bibliothèque Nationale, Paris. MS Lat. 173 f 6v. Paris/Tours, late 15th cent.
6. British Library, London. Add. MS 54782 f 107. Hastings Hours, Bruges/Ghent, before 1483.
7. British Library, London. Add. MS 35214 f 67. Hours of the Master of Claude of France, about 1500-10.
8-9. Bibliothèque Nationale, Paris. Odoric Pordenone *Le Livre de Merveilles*. Photo Bridgeman Art Library.
11. Bayerische Staatsbibliothek, Munich. Cod. Lat. 28 346 f 5. Flemish, about 1500.
12. Pierpont Morgan Library, New York. MS 399. Bruges, about 1520.
14-15. British Library, London. Add. MS 18850 f 3. Bedford Hours, French, about 1423. Photos Bridgeman Art Library.
18. The National Trust, Waddesdon Manor. MS 6, Cat. 8 f 26. Christine de Pisan, French, 15th cent.
19. British Library, London. Add. MS 17012 f 2. Book of Hours belonging to a lady at Henry VIII's court, Flemish, late 15th cent.
20 left. Biblioteca Nazionale Marciana, Venice. Benedetto Rinio *Liber de Simplicibus* f 363. Italian, early 15th cent.
20 right. Victoria and Albert Museum, London. Pliny the Elder *Historia Naturalis* Book XXVI, Sienese, about 1460. Photo E. T. Archive.
21. Sir John Soane's Museum, London. Soane Book of Hours. Flemish, about 1500. Photo E. T. Archive.
23. British Library, London. Harley MS 4431 f 81. Christine de Pisan *Cité des Dames*, Paris, 1410.
24 top. British Library, London. Yates Thompson MS 30 f 11. Hours of Laudomia de Medici, Florence, about 1502.
24 bottom. British Library, London. MS Harley 1319 f 12. French, early 15th cent. Photo Bridgeman Art Library.
27. British Library, London. Add. MS 24098 f 20v. 'Golf' Book of Hours, Bruges, about 1520.
28. Musée Condé, Chantilly. P. de Crescens *Le Rustican*, about 1460. Photo Bridgeman Art Library.
30. Musée Condé, Chantilly. MS 65/1284 f 11v. *Tres Riches Heures* of the Duke of Berry, French, 1416. Photo Giraudon.
31. British Library, London. Egerton MS 2019 f 5. Book of Hours in both French and Latin, late 15th cent.
32. Victoria and Albert Museum, London. Forster Book of Hours. Photo E. T. Archive.
34. Victoria and Albert Museum, London. Playfair Book of Hours, late 15th cent. Photo E. T. Archive.

36. British Library, London. Egerton MS 2019 f 5. Book of Hours in both French and Latin, late 15th cent.
37. British Library, London. Add MS 18855 f 92. Hours of Anne of Brittany, by Jean Bourdichon, French, late 15th cent.
39 top. British Library, London. Stowe MS 955 f 9. From a book of love poems by Pierre Sala, French, early 16th cent.
39 bottom. British Library, London. Harley MS 4431 f 145. Christine de Pisan *Cité des Dames*, Paris, 1410.
40. Bibliothèque Nationale, Paris. Gaston de Foix *Livre de la Chasse*, French, late 14th cent.
41. Holkham Hall, Norfolk. MS 307 f 20. French, 15th cent.
43. British Library, London. Add. MS 35313 f 3v. Book of Hours by the Master of James VI of Scotland, about 1510.
45. British Library, London. Add. MS 54782 f 73v. Hastings Hours, Bruges/Ghent, about 1480.
46. British Library, London. Add. MS 19720 f 288. *Rustican*, French, late 15th cent.
49. British Library, London. Add. MS 24098 f 26v. 'Golf' Book of Hours, Flemish, about 1500.
50. Pierpont Morgan Library, New York. MS 399. Bruges, about 1520.
51. British Library, London. Royal MS 14 E VI f 270. *Rustican* made for Edward VI, Bruges, 1473-1483.
53. British Library, London. Add. MS 19720 f 27. *Rustican* French, late 15th cent.
54 British Library, London. Add. MS 35313 f 3. Book of Hours by the Master of James IV of Scotland, about 1510.
54. Pierpont Morgan Library, New York. MS 399. Bruges, about 1520.
56. Fitzwilliam Museum, Cambridge. MS 165 f 46. René 1, Duke of Anjou *Le Mortifiement de vaine plaisance*, Flemish, late 15th cent.
57. British Library, London. Royal MS 18 D II f 148. John Lydgate *Troy Book*, late 15th cent.
58-59. Musée Condé, Chantilly. MS 76/1362. Hours of the Duchess of Bourgogne, about 1450. Photos Giraudon.
60. Bibliothèque Nationale, Paris. MS Lat. 873,f 21. French, late 15th cent.
61. Pierpont Morgan Library, New York. MS 6.
62. British Library, London. Add. MS 19720 f 117v. *Rustican*, French, late 15th cent.
63. British Library, London. Add. MS 18855 f 73v. Hours of Anne of Brittany, by Jean Bourdichon, French, late 15th cent.
65. Victoria and Albert Museum, London. Pliny the Elder *Historia Naturalis* Book XV, Sienese, about 1460.
66. British Library, London. Add. MS 17012 f 7. Book of Hours belonging to a lady at Henry VIII's court, Flemish, late 15th cent.
67. British Library, London. Add. MS 24098 f 25v. 'Golf' Book of Hours, Flemish, about 1500.
68. The National Trust, Waddesdon Manor. MS 19, Cat 20. French, 16th cent.
69. Pierpont Morgan Library, New York. MS 399. Bruges, about 1520.
70. British Library, London. Add. MS 18852 f 7. Hours of Joanna of Castille, Bruges, 1496-1506.
71. British Library, London. Add. MS 35313 f 4. Book of Hours by the Master of James IV of Scotland, Bruges/Ghent, about 1510.
72-3. British Library, London. MS Cotton Augustus A V f 363. *Le Trésor des Histoires*, 15th cent.
74. Bibliothèque Municipale, Lyon. MS 27 f 51. French, about 1411.
76. British Library, London. Harley MS 4431 f 128. Christine des Pisan *Cité des Dames*, Paris, 1410.
77. British Library, London. Add. MS 38126 f 7. Hours of the Virgin illuminated by various artists, Flemish, about 1500.
78. Bibliothèque Royale Albert I, Brussels. MS II 158 f 11. Bruges, 1520-1530.
80. British Library, London. Harley MS 4425 f 12v. *Roman de la Rose*, Flemish, about 1500.
81. British Library, London. Stowe MS 955 f 6. From a book of love poems by Pierre Sala, French, early 16th cent.
82. British Library, London. Egerton MS 1146 f 11. 'Hunting' Book of Hours, German or Austrian, about 1500.
83. Bibliothèque Royale Albert I, Brussels. MS 10218-19 f 6v. *Modus et Ratio*.
84. top and bottom. British Library, London. Egerton MS 1146 f 5v and 9v. 'Hunting' Book of Hours, German or Austrian, about 1500.
87. top and bottom. Biblioteca Marciana, Venice. Grimani Breviary f 7, Ghent/Bruges, 1510.
90. Pierpont Morgan Library, New York. MS 6.

91. British Library, London. Add. MS 19720 f 272v. *Rustican*, French, late 15th cent.

92. British Library, London. Add. MS 35313 f 40. Book of Hours by the Master of James IV of Scotland, Bruges/Ghent, about 1510.

93. British Library, London. Add. MS 35215 f 8v. Hours of the Virgin, French, 16th cent.

94. Bayerisches Staatsbibliothek, Munich. Cod. Lat. 28345 f 6r. Flanders, about 1500.

95. British Library, London. Add. MS 18855 f 27v. Hours of Anne of Brittany, by Jean Bourdichon, French, late 15th cent.

97. British Library, London. Add MS 27695 f 14. From a treatise on the seven vices, Italian, late 14th cent. Photo Bridgeman Art Library.

99. British Library, London. Yates Thompson MS 3 f 8. Hours of Jean Dunois, Bastard of Orleans, French, mid-15th cent.

100. British Library, London. Kings MS 9 f 9v. Book of Hours, Flemish, early 16th cent.

101. British Library, London. Royal MS 14E VI f 62. *Rustican* made for Edward VI, Bruges, 1473-1485.

102-3. British Library, London. Cotton Augustus MS A V f 345. *Le Trésor des Histoires*, 15th cent.

104 and 105. British Library, London. Add. MS 38126 f 11 and f 9. Hours of the Virgin illuminated by various artists, Flemish, about 1500.

106. British Library, London. Add. MS 17102 f 10. Book of Hours belonging to a lady at Henry VIII's court, Flemish, late 15th cent.

107. British Library, London. Add. MS 19720 f 80. *Rustican*, French, late 15th cent.

108. British Library, London. Add MS 17102 f 11. Book of Hours belonging to a lady at Henry VIII's court, Flemish, late 15th cent.

109. British Library, London. Add. MS 24098 f 29v. 'Golf' Book of Hours, Flemish, about 1500.

110. British Library, London. Add. MS 18851 f 7. Breviary of Queen Isabella of Spain, illuminations Flemish, late 15th cent.

111. British Library, London. Add. MS 24098 f 28v. 'Golf' Book of Hours, Flemish, about 1500.

112. British Library, London. Ad. MS 25695 f 10. Hours of the Virgin, French, late 15th cent.

114. top. Bodleian Library, Oxford. MS Rawl. G 98 f 49v. *The Georgics* of Virgil, Italian, 15th cent.

114. bottom. British Library, London. Add. MS 18852 f 11v. Hours of Joanna of Castille, Bruges, 1496-1506.

116. British Library, London. Add. 24098 f 27v. 'Golf' book of Hours, Flemish, about 1500.

117. Musée Condé, Chantilly. Hours of the Duchess of Bourgogne, about 1450. Photo Bridgeman Art Library.

118. British Library, London. Sloane MS 2468 f 115. Umfray Hours, French, late 15th cent.

120. British Library, London. Add. MS 18851 f 1v. Breviary of Queen Isabella of Spain, illuminations Flemish, late 15th cent.

121. British Library, London. Add. MS 18855 f 58v. Hours of Anne of Britanny, by Jean Bourdichon, French, late 15th cent.

123. British Library, London. Royal MS 14E VI f 76v. *Rustican* made for Edward VI, Bruges, 1473-1485.

124. British Library, London. Add. MS 24098 f 28v. 'Golf' Book of Hours, Flemish, about 1500.

125. British Library, London. Egerton MS 1146 f 13v. 'Hunting' Book of Hours, German or Austrian, about 1500.

126. top. British Library, London. Add. MS 35313 f 6v. Book of Hours by the Master of James VI of Scotland, Bruges/Ghent, late 15th cent.

126. bottom. Österreichischer Nationalbibliothek, Vienna. Cod 18880 f 17.

127. British Library, London. Kings MS 9 f 3v. Book of Hours, Flemish, 16th cent.

128. Pierpont Morgan Library, New York. MS 399. Bruges, about 1520.

129 top. Bodleian Library, Oxford. MS Douce 195 f 60. Guillaume de Lorris and Jean de Lutine *Roman de la Rose*, French, late 15th cent.

129 bottom. British Library, London. Yates Thompson MS 30 f 2. Hours of Laudomia de Medici, Florence, about 1502.

131. Walters Art Gallery, Baltimore. Book of Hours, Flemish, early 16th cent.

132. British Library, London. Harley MS 4375 f 151v. French, late 14th cent.

133. British Library, London. Add. MS 35215 f 97. Hours of the Virgin, French, 16th cent.

134-5. Musée Condé, Chantilly. Hours of the Duchess of Bourgogne, about 1450. Photos Giraudon.

137. Bibliothèque Nationale, Paris. MS 6185 f 51.

FURTHER READING

Grenville Astill and Annie Grant, eds., *The countryside of medieval England* (Oxford, 1988).

Richard Barber, *The Penguin guide to medieval Europe* (Harmondsworth, 1984).

H.S. Bennett, *Life on the English manor: a study of peasant conditions* (Cambridge, 1937).

Roger Boase, *The origins and meaning of courtly love* (Manchester, 1977).

T.S.R. Boase, *Death in the middle ages: mortality, judgement and remembrance* (London, 1972).

W.F. Bolton, ed., *A history of literature in the English language*, vol. I, *The middle ages* (London, 1970).

D.S. Brewer, *Chaucer* (London, 1953; revised 3rd edition, London, 1973).

D.S. Brewer, *Chaucer in his time* (London, 1963).

D.S. Brewer, *English gothic literature* (London, 1983).

John Burrow, *Medieval writers and their work: Middle English literature and its background 1100-1500* (Oxford, 1982).

William R. Cook and Ronald B. Herzman, *The medieval world view* (Oxford, 1983).

Stephen Coote, *English literature of the middle ages* (Harmondsworth, 1988).

Christopher de Hamel, *A history of illuminated manuscripts* (Oxford, 1986).

Peter Dronke, *The medieval lyric* (London, 1968).

Christopher Dyer, *Standards of living in the later middle ages* (Cambridge, 1989).

Joan Evans, ed. *The flowering of the middle ages* (London, 1966: reprinted London, 1985).

Boris Ford, ed., *The new Pelican guide to English literature* Vol. 1, Pt 1: *Chaucer and the alliterative tradition* (Harmondsworth, 1982). Vol. 1, Pt 2: *The European inheritance* (Harmondsworth, 1983).

Barbara A. Hanawalt, *The ties that bound: peasant families in medieval England* (Oxford, 1986).

John Harthan, *Books of Hours and their owners* (London, 1977).

J. Huizinga, *The waning of the middle ages* (1924: repr. Harmondsworth, 1965).

Richard Holt, *The mills of medieval England* (Oxford, 1988).

W.T.H. Jackson, *Medieval literature: a history and a guide* (London, 1967).

E.F. Jacob, *The fifteenth century 1399-1405* (Oxford, 1961).

David Knowles, *The evolution of medieval thought* (London, 1982).

C.S. Lewis, *The discarded image: an introduction to medieval and renaissance literature* (Cambridge, 1964).

H.R. Loyn, ed., *The middle ages: a concise encyclopedia* (London, 1989).

May McKisack, *The fourteenth century 1307-1399* (Oxford, 1959).

Teresa McLean, *Medieval English gardens* (London, 1981).

Stephen Medcalf, ed., *The later middle ages* (London, 1981).

G.R. Owst, *Literature and pulpit in medieval England* (Oxford, 1933; repr. Oxford, 1962).

Derek Pearsall and Elizabeth Salter, *Landscapes and seasons of the medieval world* (London, 1973).

James M. Powell, *Medieval studies: an introduction* (Syracuse, N.Y., 1976).

Edith Rickert, *Chaucer's world* (New York and London, 1948).

Beryl Smalley, *The study of the Bible in the middle ages* (Oxford, 1984).

Jonathan Sumption, *Pilgrimage* (London, 1975).

Thomas Tusser, *Five hundred points of good husbandry* (Oxford, 1984).

Rosemond Tuve, *Seasons and months: studies in a tradition of middle English poetry* (Paris, 1933; repr. Folcroft, Pa., 1971).

W. Tydeman, *The theatre in the middle ages* (Cambridge, 1978).

C. Anne Wilson, *Food and drink in Britain from the stone age to recent times* (London, 1973).

INDEX